THE SENTENCING DISPOSITIONS OF NEW YORK CITY LOWER COURT CRIMINAL JUDGES

James R. Davis

UNIVERSITY
PRESS OF
AMERICA

Copyright © 1982 by
James R. Davis

University Press of America, Inc.
P.O. Box 19101, Washington, D.C. 20036

Printed in the United States of America

Library of Congress Cataloging in Publication Data

Davis, James R., 1947-
    The sentencing dispositions of New York City lower
court criminal judges.

    Bibliography: p.
    Includes index.
    1. Sentences (Criminal procedure)--New York (N.Y.)
2. New York (N.Y.). Criminal Court (Kings County, N.Y.)
I. Title.
KFX2007.D38 1982   345.747'10722   82-45016
ISBN 0-8191-2566-0   347.47105772
ISBN 0-8191-2567-9 (pbk.)

ACKNOWLEDGMENTS

It is difficult to name everyone who has helped me to obtain the data I needed to do this research. I'd like to thank Mr. Robert Rendell, branch chief of Brooklyn Criminal Court's probation department, for arranging for the permission I needed to inspect the case folders. I'd like to thank Mr. Carmine LaFaro, chief of the clerk's office at Brooklyn Criminal Court, and his assistants, for allowing and helping me to search the adjournment books and court papers. I'd like to thank the many probation officers, legal aid attorneys, district attorneys, and judges who allowed me to interview them for long periods of time in spite of their heavy schedules. I'd like to thank some of the personnel at Brooklyn Criminal Court who gave me good advice in analyzing the data.

I'd like to thank my typist for the many pains-taking efforts she displayed in typing the final draft of this book. I'd like to especially thank my wife Roberta for her valuable suggestions in editing the final draft of this book.

TABLE OF CONTENTS

Page

List of Tables

List of Tables (continued)

LIST OF FIGURES

PREFACE

Since writing this book, I have pondered the fact that my conclusions have important implications for both criminal justice and sociology. First, my conclusion that probation officers have a great deal of power in sentencing means that judges share the power of sentencing among various actors in the system. This means that officially and formally judges sentence defendants, but informally the power of sentencing is behind the throne in an organized system of criminal justice.

Second, my conclusion that judges and probation officers are guided by a set of regularities and are consistent might be a dominant factor responsible for a smooth-running, regular, functional system.

Third, my conclusion that defendants very often receive individual attention might be important as a definition of criminal justice. Although criminal justice is difficult to define, the defendants, their social peers, legal actors, and the public might believe that justice is being practiced when they observe that cases are processed individually rather than in mass production.

Fourth, my conclusion that legal variables are more important than extra-legal variables might have policy implications. It is possible that sentencing can be objective, measured precisely, and weighted according to certain criteria rather than subjective, based on racial or ethnic categories, social class position, etc. This might be the reasoning involved in determinate sentencing, for example.

Finally, my conclusion that sentencing is a complex process, rather than a routinized process, might mean that much effort and organization enter into the sentencing dispositions of misdemeanants. Guesswork is at a minimum, because a great deal of resources and thought processes enter into the decisions.

One can speculate if the conclusions have changed since I did my research. There was a rumor circulating in the probation department that prosecutors' promises were binding and definite compared to probation officers' recommendations. I was asked to do research on this. The results showed that after controlling for many variables, and although prosecutors share the sentencing decisions, judges still favor probation officers' recommendations compared to the recommendations of prosecutors. The cases were for the years 1977 and 1978, which were later than the year for this present research.[1]

One can also ask if the results of my study are applicable to other courts. A review of the literature reveals that probation officers are not influential in all jurisdictions. Based on my experience in probation, I believe that the results of my study apply to all New York City, although I have not empirically tested this. I am certain that my results apply to many jurisdictions outside of New York City.

All this proves that research in criminal justice is problematic; it is time and place bound. Conclusions that are taken for granted can change quickly. There is nothing definite about my conclusions nor the conclusions of any other researcher. However, it is also possible for conclusions to remain the same, or to remain relatively constant. What changes and what remains constant is an empirical question. Therefore, it is essential that myself and other researchers constantly re-evaluate hypotheses, research methods and conclusions. This, after all, is the definition of science.

James R. Davis

February, 1982

---

[1]James R. Davis, "The Sentencing Dispositions of Prosecutors, Probation Officers, and Judges in a New York City Lower Criminal Court," paper presented at the American Sociological Association, New York, 1980.

Chapter I

INTRODUCTION

This research is a study of the sentencing dispositions of judges and the recommendations of probation officers at Brooklyn Criminal Court located at 120 Schermerhorn Street, Brooklyn. Brooklyn Criminal Court is mainly a lower criminal court; therefore, this research is restricted to misdemeanors and violations. This researcher will try to find out both what factors the judges and probation officers use in the sentencing process and how much weight these factors have in the sentencing process. He will try to find out to what extent judges follow probation officers' recommendations. He will attempt to find out how consistent probation officers and judges are in sentencing defendants. He will also try to find out if there is a set of regularities or patterns in sentencing. He will try to find out if defendants receive individual attention in the dispositions of their cases. He will also try to find out who is influential in the sentencing process.

The research years were from July 1, 1976 through September 30, 1978, and the cases were from the period January 1, 1972 through June 30, 1975, and from April 1, 1976 through December 31, 1976. However, a small percentage of cases preceded 1972.[1]

The methodology used was both quantitative and qualitative analysis. Three random samples were obtained from both closed cases in the probation department and court papers in closed files. Two pilot studies were conducted, namely, a review of closed probation cases and interviews with legal actors in the court to determine what variables were important for this research. The statistical methods used were path analysis and discriminant analysis. The data were analyzed on the computers at New York University's computer center, and the computer language was SPSS.[2] The methodology will be discussed further in Chapter III.

This researcher is a probation officer who is

---

[1]This is mainly because some cases from 1969, 1970 and 1971 were adjourned to 1972.

[2]Statistical Package for the Social Sciences.

1

employed at Brooklyn Criminal Court, the locus of the present research. He has been assigned to this court since March 1, 1972, although he has been a probation officer since July 1, 1970. Therefore, his powers of observation will be used as part of the methodology.

Importance of the Study

Sentencing itself has been a long neglected topic.[1] There is practically no evidence on how decisions are made to send people to jail.[2] The layman doesn't question the judge's decisions, and he doesn't know that judges are subject to idiosyncrasies.[3] Even short sentences have an effect on prisoners. One month in jail may be quite painful to prisoners.[4]

Prisoners compare sentences with one another and this can lead to a great deal of unrest. Much of the prison unrest can be attributed to unequal sentences.[5]

Conklin, based on interviews with prisoners, found that some offenders due to inconsistencies in sentence length, were occasionally motivated to commit robberies that yielded large sums of money.[6] Disparity in sentencing can make defendants bitter when they are

---

[1]George N. Pugh and Hampton Carver, "Due Process and Sentencing from Mapp to Mempa to McGautha", Texas Law Review, 1974, 49:25-29.

[2]James Eisenstein and Herbert Jacob, Felony Justice--An Organizational Analysis of Criminal Courts, Boston: Little, Brown and Company, 1977, 4.

[3]Frederick J. Gaudet, "Individual Differences in Some Sentencing Tendencies of Judges", in Glendon Shubert, Judicial Behavior--a Reader, Chicago: Rand and McNally, 1964, 352-66.

[4]Edward Eldefonso, Issues in Corrections--a Book of Readings, Beverly Hills: Glencoe Press, 1974, 289.

[5]Frank L. Morris, "The Outsider--An Alternative Role for Defense", in Herbert Jacob, Potential for Reform in Criminal Justice, Beverly Hills: Sage Publications, 1974, 303.

[6]John E. Conklin, Robbery and the Criminal Justice System, New York: J. B. Lippincott, 1972, 20.

released from prison.[1]

The Model Penal Codes state that the pre-sentence report is the greatest hope for improvement in the sentencing process.[2] Judges rarely state reasons for their decisions. Although all parts of the criminal justice system are important, sentencing decisions are crucial because this is when the defendant is told of the punishment for his crime.

Several critics have argued that the misdemeanant has been neglected in research.[3] A review of the literature on sentencing reveals that most of the studies on sentencing are either on felonies or on a combination of felonies and misdemeanors, not misdemeanors alone. More people are arrested and heard for misdemeanors and violations than for felonies.[4] Approximately one-half of all arrests are for drunkenness and disorderly conduct, and these crimes comprise the greatest bulk of cases in the lower criminal courts.[5]

Some critics have argued that our lower courts tend to dispose of cases in an assembly line manner,[6] that trials barely last more than 15 minutes,[7] and that there is little preparation of cases before the

---

[1] Andrew A. Bruce et al., The Workings of the Indeterminate Sentence--Law and the Parole System in Illinois, Montclair: Patterson Smith, 1968, 54.

[2] Leon Radzinowicz and Marvin E. Wolfgang, Crime and Justice--The Criminal in the Arms of the Law, V.II, New York: Basic Books, 1911, 14.

[3] Maureen Mileski, "Courtroom Encounters--An Observation of a Lower Criminal Court", Law and Society Review, 1971, 51:488.

[4] Lucinda Long, "Innovation in Urban Criminal Misdemeanor Courts", in Herbert Jacob, Potential for Re-Form in Criminal Justice, 123.

[5] Herbert Packer, The Limits of Criminal Sanctions, Stanford: Stanford University Press, 1968, 292.

[6] Pierce O'Donnel, Michael Churgin and Dennis E. Curtis, Towards a Just and Effective Sentencing System--Agenda for Legislative Reform, New York, Prager, 1977, 212.

[7] Task Force Report, "The Courts", in Radzinowicz and Wolfgang, 390, 392.

courts.[1] Maureen Mileski in her study of a lower criminal court observed that few misdemeanants tried to
defend themselves, and that misdemeanor courts were
mostly sentencing courts.[2] Most misdemeanants are not
paroled.[3]

A review of the literature reveals that there are
very few studies on sentencing of New York City alone
and only a few studies which have included New York
City as well as other cities across the nation. The
criminal justice system is disunified and there are
many similarities and differences among jurisdictions
in sentencing policies in American society. For these
reasons, a study of a lower criminal court in New York
City is important.

Review of the Literature

In this section there will be a review of some of
the important empirical studies on sentencing both in
American society and in other societies. The studies
chosen for analysis are mainly ones which emphasize
either some important theoretical or methodological
issue or add new knowledge to the subject of sentencing. The studies were obtained from Sociological Ab-
stracts, Index to Legal Periodicals, and various bibliog-
raphies in the literature. There will be a critique
of the various studies.

Discrimination

Many studies were concerned with discrimination
in the sentencing process. This was based on either
the ethnicity of the defendant or the offender-victim
category, or both. Some of these studies were very
early studies. For example, Thorsten Sellin collected
statistics on Detroit, and on Alabama and other states
during the period of the 1920s and concluded that Negroes were discriminated against compared to Whites in
both conviction and sentencing.[4]

Garfinkel in his study of homicide cases in North
Carolina from 1930 to 1940 concluded that a Negro who

---

[1]Laura Banfield and David Anderson, "Continuances
in the Cook County Criminal Courts", University of Chicago Law Review, 1968, 35:259-316.

[2]Mileski, 491-2.

[3]Eldefonso, 18.

[4]Thorsten Sellin, "The Negro Criminal--a Statistical Note", Annals, 1928, 149:52-64.

murdered a Negro was punished more leniently compared to Negroes who killed Whites.[1] Guy Johnson concluded that Negroes who killed other Negroes were punished more leniently compared to Negroes who killed Whites.[2]

Edward Green examined 291 burglary cases and 118 robbery cases obtained from the late 1950s in Philadelphia and concluded that although Negroes who committed crimes against other Negroes were punished more leniently compared to others, they had less serious records and a lesser number of bills of indictment.[3] Bensing and Schroeder examined 662 homicides in Cleveland for the years 1947 and 1951. They concluded that although the offender-victim category of Negro versus White was punished more severely compared to other offender-victim categories, these offenders were not discriminated against because they also faced more serious charges than others.[4]

Although the offender-victim category was controlled for in four of these studies and the ethnicity of the offender in one of these studies, the researchers did not control for more than one or two variables. Data on homicide were used in three of these studies and data on other crimes were used in two of the studies. The researchers found evidence of discrimination in three of these studies and the researchers found no evidence of discrimination in two of these studies.

Two studies by Wolfgang and Riedel also involved the offender-victim category as a variable. One study involved research on over 3000 rape convictions in 230 counties

---

[1]Harold Garfinkel, "Research Note--Inter-and Intra-Racial Homicide," Social Forces, 1949, 27:369-81.

[2]Guy Johnson, "The Negro and Crime," Annals, 1941, 217:93-104.

[3]Edward Green, "Inter= and Intra-Racial Crime Relative to Sentencing," Journal of Criminal Law and Criminology, 1964, 55:348-58.

[4]Michael Hindelang, "Equality Under the Law," in Jack L. Kuykendall and Charles Reasons, Race, Crime and Justice, Pacific Palisades: Goodyear Publisher Co., 1972, 18-9.

in 11 states for the years 1945 to 1951. The authors concluded that there was discrimination against the Negro. Among 1,265 cases in which the race of the defendant was known, nearly seven times as many Blacks compared to Whites were sentenced to death. The authors also concluded that discrimination existed against the offender-victim category of Black offender versus White victim. Black defendants whose victims were White were sentenced to death 18 times more frequently than other offender-victim categories. The researchers controlled for 24 extra-legal variables.

The other study involved 364 cases in which death sentences were imposed in Georgia for the years 1945 to 1965. Here, the researchers used discriminant analysis and controlled for many variables and concluded that the category of Negro offender versus White victim had the greatest discriminating power in sentences of death.[1]

These two studies are advanced methodologically over the earlier studies because many controls were introduced into the analysis. Discriminant analysis was used in one study, and the other study was a national study.

Peter Burke and Austin Turke conducted a study on 3,741 adults arrested in Indianapolis in 1964. The independent variables were age, race, occupational status and pre-trial status, and the dependent variable was sentence disposition. The authors concluded that the defendants in pre-trial detention received jail sentences more compared to defendants released before sentencing. Here, race had an effect opposite to expectation, since Non-Whites received preferential treatment compared to Whites.[2]

In addition to the findings on race, this study is important because of its advanced methodology. Log-

---

[1]Marvin E. Wolfgang and Marc Riedel, "Race, Judicial Discretion and the Death Penalty," Annals, 1972, 407:119-33, and "Rape, Race and the Death Penalty," American Journal of Orthopsychiatry, 1975, 45:658-68.

[2]Peter Burke and Austin Turke, "Factors Affecting Post-arrest Dispositions," Social Problems, 1975, 22:313-32.

linear methods were employed in the analysis. This is a method by which interaction can be determined for nominal levels of measurement. This is one of the few studies in sentencing in which this method is employed. This study also brought out the importance of pre-trial status as a factor in sentencing.

Discrimination can work not only in the choice of sentence, but also on sentence length for those sentenced to imprisonment. Bullock conducted a study on sentence length on 36,444 inmates in Texas. He found a close relationship between length of sentence and nature of offense, with the more serious offenses receiving longer sentences. There was no relation between length of prison sentence and number of prior convictions. Guilty pleas were associated with shorter sentences, and longer sentences were associated with offenders who committed their crimes in large cities. He controlled for non-racial factors and found that Negroes who pleaded guilty received longer sentences compared to Whites who pleaded guilty. He also found discrimination in the offender-victim category. Negroes in rape and murder cases who committed crimes against other Negroes received shorter sentences compared to Negroes who committed crimes against Whites in burglary cases.[1]

There was other important research in which discrimination was studied. However, these other studies were important not only because discrimination was the topic of research, but because other important concepts and principles were emphasized. In other words, racial and ethnic discrimination was only one theoretical orientation; one such study will be discussed.

Green conducted a study of 1,437 cases in Philadelphia for the years 1956 and 1957. He found that the nature of the present offense was the most important determinant in the sentencing process. He found the prior record was the second most important factor in sentencing. Green controlled for both seriousness and disposition of prior arrests. He found that the number

---

[1]Henry Allen Bullock, "Significance of the Racial Factor in Length of Prison Sentence," _Journal of Criminal Law, Criminology and Police Science_, 1961, 52:411-17.

of prior felony convictions was the most important determinant in prior record. In the event of no prior felony convictions, the number of prior misdemeanors resulting in jail was used as criterion in sentencing. In the event of no prior misdemeanors resulting in jail the number of prior misdemeanors resulting in lesser penalties was used as a criterion in sentencing. In no case was the number of arrests used in determining the sentence of the defendant.

Green also found that the number of bills of indictment had an effect on sentencing. He found that men received harsher sentences compared to women. He found that guilty pleas yielded heavier sentences compared to trial by jury, a finding which was surprising when reviewing the literature. He also found that differences among presecutors were not crucial in sentencing. He also found that defendants on bail received prison less often than defendants in remand before sentencing.

He also found no discrimination against Negroes, because the Negroes met the criteria for imprisonment more than the Whites. He found no discrimination between Northern-born and Southern-born Negroes.

Green also studied consistency in sentencing. Consistency can be defined as the handling of similar cases in similar ways. He found that judges were guided by certain regularities in the sentencing process. Inconsistencies, Green concluded, were in the middle ranges of serious cases. Judges were most consistent at the extreme ends of the serious cases, in the least serious and most serious cases. Green also studied cases from two courts, bail court and prison court. He found that only 15.1% of the defendants convicted in bail court campared to 78.4% in prison court received prison sentences.[1]

Green used the statutory law in scaling the seriousness of present and past arrests. For example, offenses against the public and against property were less serious than crimes against persons.

---

[1]Edward Green, Judicial Attitudes in Sentencing-- a Study of the Factors Underlying the Sentencing Practices of the Criminal Court in Philadelphia, New York: MacMillan, 1961.

The degree of violation of personality was considered most serious in statutory offenses.[1]

The statutory penalties are not the only way to scale seriousness of crime. Green didn't control for SES, an important variable. He didn't use sentence length as a dependent variable. He used non-parametric methods, which usually is less informative than multiple regression analysis. For example, Green concluded that the seriousness of present crimes was more important than prior record but it is difficult to find out how much effect both variables had in the sentencing process. However, Green should be commended for introducing controls for seriousness of prior arrests and seriousness of prior convictions, an innovation in the literature.

Green has been criticized by other researchers. For example, Levine has criticized Green for combining the category of probation with those who received jail for three months or less. Although Levine doesn't elaborate on this point, one can speculate that perhaps Levine believed that jail and probation were two distinct categories in which different variables might have a different effect. Perhaps Levine believed that one loses some important conclusions by combining these two distinct categories. One can question this, because these categories have been combined, for example, in cases of split sentence of probation and jail.

Levine also demonstrated that Green misinterpreted the differences between Blacks and Whites with one or more prior arrests. Levine also questioned his combination of zero and one arrest into one category. This criticism can be questioned. Levine also criticized his conclusion of consistency among the judges in the extreme ends of the gravity scale of offenses. Levine reinterpreted Green's data and concluded that there was more variation at the extreme ends of the scale than Green realized, thus weakening Green's conlusions.[2]

---

[1]Martin A. Levine, Urban Politics and the Criminal Courts, Chicago: University of Chicago Press, 1977, 247-8.

[2]Ibid.

Green was also criticized by John Hogarth. Hogarth criticized Green for imputing attitudes about judges on the basis of objective criteria used in sentencing rather than measuring these attitudes directly. Hogarth believed that this same criticism applied to other researchers in addition to Green.[1]

Conflict Theory

Discrimination can operate on other variables besides race. It can operate on social class or on occupation. Discrimination in sentencing based on race, occupation, and social class can test the conflict theory of criminology, a theory which proposes that defendants are sentenced with discrimination on the basis of extra-legal criteria rather than on the basis of objective, legal variables. A few examples will be presented which directly or indirectly test the conflict theory.

Swigert and Farrell studied 444 cases of murder for the years January 1, 1955 through December 31, 1975, obtained from the records of a diagnostic clinic attached to a court. They used path analysis to analyze their data. They introduced the concept of "normal primitive" into their analysis. It was a concept based on a popular image of defendants, stereotypes based on race and class. Defendants labeled "normal primitive" were not only Black and from lower-class backgrounds, but they were also less educated, older and less intelligent compared to others. The classification "normal primitive" was not associated with only one racial type. They were mainly from lower-class backgrounds.

The defendants classified as "normal primitive" were denied access to bail, trial by jury, and access to private counsel. The award of bail, trial by jury, and access to legal counsel were the resources associated with less severe dispositions. The researchers concluded that race was not directly associated with final disposition, and that although both seriousness of offense and prior record influenced outcomes, minority groups were not penalized because of these factors. Rather the designation "normal primitive" worked to deny these defendants so designated access to resources, e.g., counsel, bail, trial by jury, which indirectly affected final dispositions. A comparison of the findings with other findings of the same kind revealed that the results held up even when controlling for geographical

---

[1]John Hogarth, Sentencing as a Human Process, Toronto: University of Toronto Press, 1971, 8.

area, time frames, and data sources.[1]

Chiricos and Waldo tested the conflict theory. They examined prison sentences for 10,488 criminals in three states, Florida, North Carolina, and South Carolina, for 17 offenses. Even after controlling for numerous variables, including prior record and demographic characteristics of the defendants, the zero-order correlations between SES and sentence length were very low, or negative, accounting for no more than 2% to 4% of the variance. The researches used both beta-coefficients and multiple correlations to analyse their data. They concluded that there was no support for the conflict theory in criminology which espoused discrimination against members of the lower SES classes.[2]

Chiricos and Waldo have been criticized by other researchers. For example, Andrew Hopkins questioned the study methodologically, especially the researchers' treatment of SES in continuous terms, rather than in dichotomous terms, and their exclusion of data from upper-middle classes in the sample.[3]

Charles Reasons has also criticized Chiricos and Waldo. Reasons argued that the researchers had only partially tested the conflict perspective. He also noted that the researchers only had lower-class defendants in their sample, and therefore, their research was only one of "within-class distinctions" rather than "between-class distinctions". He also criticised Chiricos and Waldo for failing to grasp the true relationship between idology, "world view", and the

[1]Victoria Lynn Swigert and Ronald A. Farrell, Murder, Inequality and the Law--Differential Treatment in the Legal Process, Lexington: Lexington Books, 1976, and "Normal Homicides and the Law", American Sociological Review, February, 1977, 42:16-32.

[2]Theodore G. Chiricos and Gordon Waldo, "Socioeconomic Status and Criminal Sentencing--An Empirical Assessment of a Conflict Proposition", American Sociological Review, December, 1975, 40:753-72.

[3]Andrew Hopkins, "Is There a Class Bias in Sentencing?", American Sociological Review, February, 1977, 42:176-77.

practice of science, which he believed was important in understanding conflict theory.[1]

Alan J. Lizotte conducted research on two random samples of cases in Chicago, heard during the years of 1971-72. The first sample consisted of 220 cases processed through 15 Chicago trial courts in 1971 and a second sample consisted of 596 cases processed in which a grand jury returned an indictment making a total sample of 816 cases. The dependent variable was sentence length, and the independent variables were occupation, race, prior arrests in Chicago, evidence, seriousness of case, not making bail, bail amount and legal counsel's degree of success in sentencing. Prison sentence length was coded as the average of the minimum and maximum sentences in months, and probation and acquittal were both coded zero prison sentences. Path analysis was used to analyze the data.

The findings indicated that the more serious cases received longer prison sentences. Surprisingly, those with no attorney received shorter prison sentences compared to those with private, non-regular attorneys; public defenders were associated with the longest prison sentences. Lizotte believed that defendants with no lawyer had prior experience in criminal justice and were wise in the ways of the system, thus facilitating favorables outcomes for them. Finally, not making bail was associated with longer prison sentences.

Lizotte also substituted the numerical mean values of such variables as bail, type of attorney, etc. from the cases of higher SES classes to the cases of Black and White laborers in the lower SES classes, and reanalyzed the data, and concluded that both Black and White laborers were twice as likely as higher SES White proprietors to remain incarcerated before sentencing, and thus more likely to receive longer prison sentences compared to white proprietors. He also concluded that White laborers were given longer sentences compared to Black laborers, perhaps indicating that judges considered Black laborers' crimes more normative to Black culture and less serious compared to White laborers' crimes.

---

[1]Charles E. Reasons, "On Methodology, Theory and Ideology," American Sociological Review, February, 1977, 42: 177-81.

Lizotte also found that jail was determined by the seriousness of the case, type of attorney, prior record and evidence. He found that not making bail was determined by type of attorney, amount of bail, evidence, race and occupation. These variables worked indirectly on sentence length, since making or not making bail indirectly affected sentence length.

Lizotte concluded that the results of his analysis indicated strong evidence for the conflict theory. Based on the analysis of the data, the fact that Whites and Blacks from lower SES classes compared to high SES Whites both stayed in jail longer before sentencing and received longer sentences, even when controlling for relevant variables, Lizotte concluded that the courts in Chicago discriminated against defendants in punishment based on the factors of race, occupation and class.[1]

Another study conducted by Stuart Nagel seems to show evidence in support of the conflict theory. Nagel conducted a study of 846 assault cases and 1,103 larceny cases on the state level and 196 assault and 785 larceny cases on the federal level in 1962. This was a nationwide study involving 50 states. He found that the indigent were less likely than the non-indigent to be granted probation or suspended sentence, even when controlling for seriousness of offense and prior record. However, he did find that although the Negroes were imprisoned more than the Whites and were less likely to receive a grand jury indictment, they received shorter prison sentences than the Whites, possibly due to the smaller amounts they had stolen. The indigent were found guilty more often than the non-indigent.

He found that there was a difference between urban, northern courts, southern, rural courts and federal, state courts. For example, urban, northern courts were less likely to imprison for larceny and more likely to imprison for assault compared to southern, rural courts, which imprisoned more for larceny and less for assault. The Negro defendant was discriminated against more in the southern than in the northern court. Imprisonment in the rural, southern courts seemed to be harsher compared to imprisonment in the northern, urban courts. The

[1]Alan J. Lizotte, "Extra-Legal Factors in Chicago's Criminal Courts--Testing the Conflict Model of Criminal Justice", Social Problems, June, 1978, 25:564-80.

federal courts granted probation and suspended sentence more than the state courts. Nagel concluded that the indigent were discriminated against more than the Negro in the administration of Justice.[1]

Comparative Studies

There were two studies in which sentences were compared in different cities in the United States. These studies are important because one can ascertain what factors are unique and what factors are uniform in the sentencing process. One can tell if certain cultural and social factors associated with different cities, e.g., organization of the court, public policy, etc. enter into the sentencing process.

Martin Levine conducted a comparative study of the sentencing process in two cities, Minneapolis and Pittsburgh, in the early 1960s. Analysis of case records, observation, and interviews were used as methods. The final samples consisted of 4,324 cases in Pittsburgh and 2,513 cases in Minneapolis. Levine concluded that sentencing was more lenient in Pittsburgh compared to Minneapolis. Both Whites and Blacks received probation and shorter prison terms in Pittsburgh compared to Minneapolis, even when controlling for prior record, type of plea, and age. However, Whites received probation more frequently compared to Blacks in both cities, and in Minneapolis Whites received shorter prison sentences compared to Blacks, and Blacks received shorter prison sentences in Pittsburgh compared to Whites.

Levine concluded that the political system was the factor associated most with these differences in sentencing. First, Minneapolis tends to be middle-class in educational background and occupation and Pittsburgh tends to be more working-class, an industrial city. Second, the judges' backgrounds reflect this difference between the two cities. Judges from Minneapolis are middle-class Protestant in background compared to judges in Pittsburgh, who are more working-class in origin. Third, these differential backgrounds between judges seem to reflect differences in attitudes toward offenders. Judges in Minneapolis are oriented toward society and the law, but judges in Pittsburgh

---

[1]Stuart Nagel, "Disparities in Criminal Procedures," University of California Law Review, August, 1964, 14: 1271-1305.

are oriented toward the defendant, and empathize more with the defendant, compared to judges in Minneapolis. Fourth, these attitudes tend to consciously or unconsciously work toward differential sentencing patterns in the two cities.

Since judges in Pittsburgh advance occupationally via the political machine, they are oriented toward the individual. Levine compared the two cities politically, and stated that Pittsburgh had a formally partisan and highly centralized city government, compared to Minneapolis, which had a formally non-partisan and structurally fragmented city government.[1]

Eisenstein and Jacob conducted a comparative study of the courtrooms in three cities, Baltimore, Detroit and Chicago. They studied 4,371 court cases for the years 1972-73. They used multivariate analysis, including discriminant analysis, to analyze their data. They also observed court proceedings. They studied not only the sentencing process, but also plea bargaining, arraignment and other aspects of the criminal justice system. Some of their generalizations were that plea-bargaining was not universally prevalent and did not always lead to lighter sentences compared to bench trials, Blacks were not always treated worse than Whites, public defenders were not always less effective than retained counsel, and jailed defendants were not always consistently convicted more than those who were released before trial.

Specifically, there were differences in sentencing among the three cities. For defendants not sent to jail Baltimore relied heavily on suspended sentences while Chicago and Detroit relied on probation. Chicago used jail heavily as a sentence. The variables associated with prison varied among the three cities. The original charge and the identity of the courtroom explained much of the variance in all three cities. The identity of the courtroom was defined by the authors as the distinctive decisions and norms concerning criminal justice output made as a result of interaction among the legal actors in a particular courtroom.

---

[1]Martin A. Levine, "Urban Politics and Judicial Behavior", Journal of Legal Studies, 1972, 1:193-221, and Urban Politics and the Criminal Courts.

These courtrooms were described as "workgroups". In Baltimore and Detroit, defendants' characteristics were important in sentencing decisions, but this was not true in Chicago. In Detroit, defendants on bail received probation more than defendants in jail before sentencing. In each city, different criteria were applied in each courtroom. The authors concluded that Baltimore imposed the most severe sentences and Detroit the most lenient sentences.

The researchers also examined sentence length. They found that the original charge was the most important factor associated with sentence length. Other factors of lesser importance were defendants' characteristics, dispositional mode and stage, and the identity of the courtroom.

The authors concluded that it was difficult to make any general conclusions about the sentencing process not only among all three cities, but even in each separate city.

Eisenstein and Jacob introduce an organizational and symbolic interaction approach to their research. The workshops in which the legal actors worked facilitated interaction which resulted in developing norms which were associated with the outcomes. These workshops were distinctive and specific to each courtroom, even in the same city. The identity of the courtroom and the workshop in which the legal actors worked were very important for sentencing outcomes. The researchers have moved beyond a simple analysis of data obtained from case records to a broad theoretical orientation.[1]

Probation Officer as

Dependent Variable

There have been few studies in which the factors probation officers use to determine their recommendations have been the topic of research. The probation officer is seen as one agent in the criminal justice process, but in many jurisdictions, he is a very important agent. His influence, especially in the lower

---

[1]James Eisenstein and Herbert Jacob, _Felony Justice--an Organizational Analysis of Criminal Courts_, and "Sentences and Other Sanctions in the Criminal Courts of Baltimore, Chicago and Detroit", _Political Science Quarterly_, December, 1975, 90:617-37.

criminal courts, has not been studied very much. Two studies are presented here as examples. One study is confined to New York City and the other study is confined to Canada.

Herbert Langerman condicted research for the years September 1, 1971 through August 31, 1972 on a random sample of 1,149 cases in four boroughs, excluding Staten Island. Fifty-three probation officers were interviewed and presented questionnaires. Three crime categories, namely possession of heroin, simple assault and petty larceny were analyzed. Females, youthful offenders, multiple charges, and fines as dispositions were excluded. The dispositions of conditional and unconditional discharge were combined. Analysis of variance and covariance were used to analyze the data. Sixteen hypotheses were presented for each of the three crimes, a total of 48 hypotheses. These hypotheses were grouped into clusters; for example, background characteristics of defendants and probation officers, political orientation of the officers, professional, bureaucratic orientation of the officers, etc.

Out of a total of 48 hypotheses, only 13 were accepted. Most of the background characteristics of offenders and officers, including race, were rejected. Some of Langerman's conclusions were that probation officers were more likely to hold recommendations similar to their best friends rather than to other probation officers, and conservative or middle-of-the-road officers were likely to be more severe than liberal officers.

Langerman also found that the number of arrests played a key role in recommendations. This interacted with type of crime. For example, in assault cases, probation officers were lenient up to five arrests, but were severe after that; however, they were severe with less than five arrests for heroin and petit larceny. Langerman concluded that the number of arrests was the most important determinant of the probation officers' recommendations.[1]

Although this was the first study of probation officers' recommendations in a lower-criminal court,

---

[1]Herbert Langerman, "Determinants of Probation Officers' Presentence Recommendations:, unpublished dissertation for Ph.D., New York University, 1976.

it only included three crime categories. Langerman excluded youthful offenders and females from his study.
He also excluded many other variables, such as pre-
trial status and offender-victim categories.

Hagan conducted a study of 765 cases from 17 cities
in a western province of Ontario for the period from
February 1, 1973 to June 1, 1973. Two samples were
studied and compared, 507 cases with a probation recommendation and 247 cases without a probation recommendation. Hagan distributed questionnaires to probation officers and used path analysis to analyze his
data. He developed three theoretical orientations,
namely, conflict theory, symbolic interaction, and organizational theory. He included both legal and extra-
legal variables. The independent variables were number
of prior convictions, seriousness of offense, number of
charges, race, SES, and two new variables, perceived
demeanor of offender, and evaluation of success prospects. The two dependent variables were recommendations
of probation officers and disposition of the judge.

Hagan formulated three hypotheses, namely, 1) officers'
success prospects will be more influential in the model
with probation officers' recommendations, 2) the probation officers will use extra-legal variables in forming
evaluations of success prospects when recommendations are
presented, and 3) race will be most important when probation officers make a recommendation. All three hypotheses were confirmed.

Hagan also concluded that all three theoretical
orientations were supported with the possibility of
synthesis of all perspectives. The perceived demeanor
of the offender and evaluation of success prospects
were found important in the sample with probation recommendations, supporting the symbolic interactionist
perspective. Race and SES were found important in probation officers' recommendations, thus supporting the
conflict perspective. Hagan believed that the organizational arrangements in which probation officers were em-
powered to make recommendations were directly or indirectly important for the use of extra-legal variables
in final disposition.[1]

_____

[1]John Hagan, "The Social and Legal Construction of
Criminal Justice"--a Survey of Pre-Sentence Process",
Social Problems, 1975, 38:620-37.

Judicial Background and Attitudes

Many of the empirical studies have omitted the background factors of judges, as well as their attitudes on punishment as determinants in sentencing decisions. This omission also applies to other legal actors in the sentencing process; for example, probation officers. Studies combining both background factors and attitudes together might yield more explanatory power in the sentencing decision than studies excluding such factors. Two studies, both in Canada, are discussed. One study combines both attitudes and background factors and the other study focuses on attitudes. The comparative study by Levine of Pittsburgh and Minneapolis already discussed also included background factors of judges in sentencing decisions.[1]

Hogarth interviewed 71 full time magistrates in Canada in 1966. He also administered questionnaires to them and analyzed case records. He used multivariate statistical analysis, including factor analysis and discriminant analysis to analyze the data.

Hogarth concluded that there was a complex relationship between attitudes and constraints on one hand, and sentencing practices of magistrates on the other. Magistrates were inconsistent among each other, but consistent among themselves. That is, magistrates treated similar cases in similar ways in their own caseload; they applied the same set of standards or guidelines to their own cases. However, each magistrate had a different set of standards for similar cases. Some of the conclusions about attitudes can be summarized. For example, magistrates with low reformation scores tended to personalize the cause of crime around such simple notions as lack of intelligence and alcoholism. Punitive-oriented magistrates were concerned with stricter laws while treatment-oriented magistrates were concerned with more flexible laws. Magistrates who had extreme attitudes at either end of the punitive scale tended to approach the decision making process in a simple way; on the other hand, magistrates who believed in reformation were more complex in their cognitive processes and actually searched for more information in more complex ways compared to others.

---

[1]Levine, Urban Politics and the Criminal Courts.

19

The background factors of magistrates were also important. Magistrates' attitudes reflected the communities from which they came. Magistrates from professional families attached more weight to reformation compared to magistrates from working-class backgrounds who were more punitive in their attitudes. This finding is in disagreement with Levine's finding, which found working-class backgrounds of judges in Pittsburgh to be associated with more lenient sentences compared to higher-class judges in Minneapolis,who were more punitive.[1] Years of experience on the bench, Hogarth concluded, were associated with a belief in deterrence. Urban magistrates were more oriented toward deterrence and retribution and less toward reformation compared to rural magistrates.

The majority of magistrates considered family background, criminal record, and employment record as essential in sentencing offenders. Also important for some magistrates were the premeditation and culpability of the offenders. The nature of the offense was very important in sentencing. The degree of remorse shown by the offender was also important. Important as factors in sentence length were the criminal record, age of offender, occupation, and number of counts in the indictment.

Hogarth found that pre-sentence reports from probation officers were used only in about 18% of the cases, and these reports were only used in unusual cases. Presentence reports did not necessarily result in closer agreement between judge and probation officer.[2]

Hagan conducted a study in Alberta, Canada on 161 incarcerated offenders and mailed questionnaires to 36 judges. He used path analysis with interaction terms to analyze his data. He concluded that judges concerned with law and order sentence offenders primarily on the basis of the legal definition of crime. Those less concerned with law and order sentence not only on the basis of the seriousness of the offense, but also on race, prior record and number of charges against the offender. This latter group was also more lenient to minority offenders compared to other judges.

---

[1]Ibid.

[2]Hogarth.

Hagan concluded that sentencing studies should combine Hogarth's judicial attitudes with Green's legal and extra-legal variables.[1]

Methodology

Some of the researchers discussed so far have used non-parametric techniques, such as chi-square, and others have used advanced multivariate analysis, such as factor analysis and discriminant analysis. One study will be discussed in which the researchers studied interaction effects among the variables to analyze the data. Although Hagan[2] studied interaction effects also, the researchers in the following study made use of interaction to a greater extent than in previously discussed studies.

Tiffany, Avichai, and Peter analyzed 1,248 cases in four crime catagories, namely, bank robbery, auto theft, interstate transportation of forged securities and miscellaneous forgery for the years 1967 and 1968 in 89 federal district courts. These cases were all the result of either bench trials or jury trials. They used regression, non-additive, probit and interaction models to analyze their data.

The researchers concluded that the crime factor had the greatest impact on sentencing. Prior record and type of conviction had a strong effect on sentencing, but weaker than the crime factor. They found that race, age and counsel had a weak effect on sentencing when analyzed separately or together. There was a strong interaction between crime and prior record, crime and type of conviction, and between type of conviction and type of lawyer. They found a moderately strong relationship between race and prior record. They found a strong interaction between crime-trial and crime-record, and no interaction between type of conviction and prior record. In support of the interaction between crime-trial and crime-record, a more severe

[1] John Hagan, "Law, Order and Sentencing, a Study of Attitudes in Action", Social Problems, 1975, 38: 374-84.

[2] Ibid.

penalty was imposed on those who were ocnvicted on a jury trial with no prior record compared to those who were convicted on a bench trial with a strong prior record. The authors concluded that the strong interaction between race and prior record and type of conviction and type of lawyer were both due to racial discrimination.

The researchers analyzed one crime, bank robbery, separately. They found that prior record and type of conviction were important here. The effect of age was found to be stronger here compared to other crimes. Race had an impact for first offenders only. Defendants represented by retained counsel received more favorable sentences compared to those represented by appointed counsel.[1]

Critique

Three critiques of sentencing studies will be discussed here. Jack Kuykendall and Charles Reasons concluded that researchers who had found no evidence of ethnic discrimination used data from the north, used more controls, used newer data, and used property crimes in their studies, compared to those who found evidence of discrimination. On the other hand, those researchers who found evidence of discrimination used southern data and data exclusively on homicide compared to those who found no evidence of discrimination.[2]

Hagan reviewed 21 studies on sentencing, some of them discussed in this research, and found that extra-legal factors explained no more than 5% of the variance. He also criticized the frequent reliance on tests of significance. He reanalyzed some data from these studies and found some results significant and some non-significant, contradicting the results of the researchers. For example, he reanalyzed Nagel's data on federal cases and found that differences between indigent and non-idigent weren't significant with

---

[1]Lawrence P. Tiffany, Yakov Avichai and Geoffrey W. Peter, "A Statistical Analysis on Sentencing in Federal Courts--Defendants Convicted After Trial", 1967-68, Journal of Legal Studies, 1975, 4:369-96.

[2]Kuykendall and Reasons, Race, Crime, Justice, 318-19.

controls for prior record. He also reanalyzed the data of Nagal and found that none of the correlations were as high as tau-b=.05. He also concluded that most of the studies under criticism used capital cases, which were only a very small part of the criminal cases.[1]

Nagel and Neef have warned us of some pitfalls in analyzing court records which can lead one to conclude that racial disparities don't exist when they do, and that racial disparaities exist when they don't. They show how equal sentences for Blacks and Whites can be unequal when controls for ethnicity of the judge, type of charge, prior record, social class, geographical region, legal actors, etc., are introduced. For example, Blacks and Whites in Atlanta, Georgia, each received an average sentence length of two years, but Black judges were sentencing Black defendants to one year and White defendants to three years, and White judges were sentencing Black defendants to three years and White defendants to one year. Other examples are used to explain the disparities.[2]

Summary

In this chapter, a statement of the research questions was presented. The importance of the study was indicated. It was stated that there was very little empirical work on either the lower criminal courts or on New York City. A review of the literature indicated some types of theoretical and empirical issues involved in sentencing studies. The conclusions from many studies showed contradictory results, even in the same study; for example, in the case of racial discrimination. Advanced statistical methods, such as factor analysis and discriminant analysis were used in some studies, and non-parametric techniques, such as chi-square analysis, were used in other studies. Many studies were criticized theoretically and methodologically.

---

[1]John Hagan, "Extra-legal Attributes and Criminal Sentences--An Assessment of a Sociological Viewpoint", Law and Society Review, 1974, 8:357-83.

[2]Stuart Nagel and Marian Neef, "Racial Disparities That Supposedly Don't Exist--Some Pitfalls in the Analysis of Court Records", Notre Dame Lawyer, October, 1976, 52:87-94.

One can conclude from the review of the literature that although some generalizations apply through-
out, such as the choice of variables in sentencing
studies, e.g., pre-trial status, prior record, nature
of charge, etc., more severe sanctions for serious
prior record, etc., it would be difficult to formulate
general principles in reference to factors affecting
all sentencing dispositions, since every city and
jurisdiction and every court in every city is unique
and can show unique results.

In Chapter II, the actual research questions will
be presented in view of some important theoretical
perspectives and in view of some of the strengths and
weaknesses of past research.

Chapter II

THEORETICAL PERSPECTIVES

AND RESEARCH QUESTIONS

In this chapter, there will be a discussion of the theoretical issues on which the research is based. The present research will be compared to some of the research presented in Chapter I. The choice of variables used in this research will be presented. The research questions will be formulated in view of some of the theoretical strengths and weaknesses of prior research.

A review of the literature indicated three classes of variables. One class consisted of legal variables, such as pre-trial status, number of arrests, number of convictions, seriousness of charge, etc. Another class consisted of personal attributes, such as age, sex, race, ethnicity, education, income. A third class consisted of relationships, such as the offender-victim category, or legal service. All three classes of variables are used in this research. Sometimes in the literature relations and personal attributes are combined into one class, extra-legal variables. These three classes of variables are not mutually exclusive; there is much overlapping; for example, age is both a legal variable and a personal attribute.

Very often the use of variables is restricted to the theoretical and research questions posed in the study. Therefore, no two studies will necessarily have the identical list of variables. Later in this chapter, the actual list of variables and the reasons for the choice of them will be presented.

Discrimination

After reviewing the literature in Chapter I, one finds that racial discrimination is an important perspective in sentencing studies. Some researchers found evidence of radial discrimination and some researchers did not, and some researchers showed mixed results. Racial discrimination can operate on the basis of the ethnicity of the defendant, the ethnicity of the victim, or the offender-victim category. These three variables can also operate in interaction with other variables. Some researchers showed that when a Negro commits a

crime against another Negro, he is punished more
leniently than when he commits a crime against a White.
The reasoning behind this is that as long as crime is
confined to the ghetto or to a member of a minority
group, this is considered less serious than when a
crime spreads out to a white neighborhood or is committed against a member of the White majority.

Few of the researchers discussed in Chapter I emphasized the offender-victim category of White vs. White
or White vs. Negro. These two latter offender-victim
categories are used in this research.

Research on discrimination can determine if a
double-standard of justice is employed in sentencing.
A double standard of justice means that differential
treatment is imposed on the basis of race. Many members of minority groups are hostile because a perceived
or real double standard of justice exists in other areas
of criminal justice. For example, many members of minority groups are hostile to police in their neighborhood
because of the double standard of justice that many police practice in protecting the ghetto neighborhoods.
Very often police will turn their heads on some crimes
in the ghetto or will use force to apprehend an offender; in White neighborhoods the police concentrate on
apprehending more criminals and will respect victims
and use no force on the offender. Other examples of a
double standard of justice allegedly exist in pre-trial
status, the granting of bail, and the appointment of
counsel.

Discrimination can operate in other areas besides
race. Discrimination can operate on the basis of sex,
age, and marital status. All these variables are used
in this research. Some judges, for example, may be more
lenient towards younger defendants or to married defendants compared to older or single defendants.

The ethnicity of the defendant, the ethnicity of
the victim, the offender-victim categories, and interaction terms with ethnicity are used in this research
to test for discrimination in sentencing.

Social Class Bias

Some of the researchers have revealed that social
class bias can be just as discriminatory as racial
bias in sentencing. Social class can have a strong
effect on sentencing dispositions. Judges and other
legal actors can discriminate directly on the basis of

26

social class, both consciously and unconsciously, just
as they can in the case of race. In addition to social
class bias, the disadvantage of a lower SES can affect
sentencing indirectly. The poor, lower SES defendants
are disadvantaged because they can't afford the resources which are believed to be associated with favorable
sentencing outcomes, namely, bail, private counsel,
etc. Some of the researchers reviewed in Chapter I
concluded that denial of bail, type of counsel, pre-
trial status, and type of plea can indirectly affect
sentencing outcomes. For example, defendants who can
afford bail may get more lenient sentences compared to
defendants who can't afford bail because defendants on
bail very often have the time and resources to fight
their cases; they also may receive favorable dispositions at arraignment and conviction.

However, as Lizotte points out, although lower
SES classes have less access to resources, they may
have more experience in the criminal justice system;
they may have more friends and relatives who are more
experienced in the system. This can be positive for
them in gaining favorable dispositions. They can use
their experience to gain advantages in the system.
Lizotte found that those with no attorney received
slightly shorter prison sentences compared to others.[1]
However, pre-trial status and type of counsel are used
in this research. Type of conviction is not used because of the small number of defendants who were sentenced on the basis of a trial.

Although pre-trial status and type of counsel are
important in sentencing, their impact is open to empirical investigation. Many researchers have found
evidence that defendants out of remand do better both
before and after sentencing. Some have concluded that
defendants with private counsel do better than defendants with public defenders.[3] However, much of the evidence is contradictory. Oaks and Lehman, for example,
reported in their study in Chicago that public

---

[1]Lizotte.

[2]Lewis R. Katz, et. al., Justice is the Crime--
Pre-trial Delays in Felony Cases, Cleveland, Press of
Case Western University, 1972, 151, 207.

[3]Stephen R. Bing and Stephen Rosenfield, The
Lower Criminal Courts of Metropolitan Boston, Boston:
Lawyers Committee for Rights Under Law, 1970, 32-34.

defenders obtained probation for their clients about twice as often as other types of counsel.[1] It is also possible for type of counsel to have no effect on sentencing.

. Social class as a variable can be used in sentencing studies to test the conflict theory of criminology, as developed by Chambliss and Seidman and others. Lizotte states:

> Conflict theorists assert that the social characteristics of defendants, such as race, and socio-economic status, are important in determining sentencing in the criminal courts...conflict theory states that our legal system does not apply the law impartially with regard to social class, occupation and race.[2]

How is social class defined? Weber has defined social class:

> A 'class' is any group of persons occupying the same class status.[3]

Weber defines "class status":

> The term 'class status' will be applied to the typical probability that a given state of a) provisions with goods, b) external conditions of life, and c) subjective satisfaction or frustration will be possessed by an individual or group. These probabilities define class status in so far as they are dependent on the kind and extent of control or lack of it which the individual has over goods or services, and existing probabilities of their exploitation for the attainment

---

[1]Dallin Oakes and Warren Lehman, "Lawyers for the Poor", in Abraham Blumberg, The Scales of Justice, New York: Aldine, 1970.

[2]Lizotte, 564-5.

[3]Max Weber, The Theory of Social and Economic Organization, translated by M. Henderson and Talcott Parsons, New York: Free Press, 1947, 424.

of income or receipts within a given
economic order.[1]

Thus, for Weber, class is defined as the life chances
an individual has to acquire economic goods, and the
subjective state of satisfaction associated with this.

Weber continues:

> Only persons who are completely
> unskilled, without property and
> dependent on employment without
> regular occupation, are in a
> strictly identical class status.
> Transitions from one class status
> to another vary greatly in fluidity
> and the ease with which an indivi-
> dual can enter the class.[2]

For Weber, there is a class which is composed of identical persons who have little or no chance of escap-
ing from their circumstances.

The defendants who come to Brooklyn Criminal Court
very often resemble the "identical class status" which
Weber talks about. They are poor; many of them receive
public assistance, and have been on welfare for years.
They are mostly unskilled, possessing no definite
working skills due to lack of training or other reasons.
They depend very much on low-level employment on an
occasional basis to survive. Many offenders who are
eligible for welfare don't receive it either because they
don't understand how to go about getting it or because
they live in the street without any home, or relatives,
or friends to help them. Many of them have revealed
to this researcher that they are psychologically frus-
trated.

Weber goes on:

> The term of 'social status' will be
> applied to a typically effective claim
> to positive or negative privilege with
> respect to one or more of the following
> bases: a) mode of living, b) a formal
> process of education which may consist

---

[1]Weber,

[2]Ibid., 425.

in empirical or rational training at the acquisition of the corresponding modes of life, or c) on the prestige of both or of occupation.[1]

Lower SES defendants are largely without formal education; some can't read or write on a minimal level. Many have language difficulties. Many don't have a regular occupation. Their mode of living, in Weber's terms would imply "negative privilege". Many of them are stigmatized by society. Many defendants live under poverty conditions, in ghetto areas, in homes that are ready to fall apart, infested with rats and roaches, without proper sanitary facilities. Many of their neighborhoods are just as bad; they are crime-infested, with drug problems, health problems, and unemployment.

Marx also talks about class. For Marx, class was mainly an economic category applicable to many social formations. Under capitalism, according to Marx, the two principal classes are the capitalists, the class with property, and the poletariat, the class without property. The defendants who come to Brooklyn Criminal Court hardly fit into either the capitalist or proletariat classes. Virtually no defendant owns any means of production, e.g., capital, machinery, etc. They would hardly fit into the proletariat class because most of them are unemployed, or work on low-level, sporadic jobs, and mainly subsist on welfare.

Although for Marx the captialists and proletariat are the two principal classes in society, he talks unfavorably about the "lumpenproletariat, this scum of depraved elements from all classes with headquarters in the big cities".[2] It seems that many of the defendants would fit into the "lumpenproletariat" class in a Marxian sense because of their unemployment, criminal records, and the stigma attributed to them by society. Many of them are at the bottom of society.

Chiricos and Waldo in their research on the relation between SES and sentence length found no basis for

---

[1]Weber, 428.

[2]Karl Marx and Frederick Engels, "Preface to the Peasant War in Germany", in Selected Works, New York: International Publishers, 1968, 243.

support of the conflict model.[1] It is very difficult
to ascertain the effect of socio-economic status of
defendants on sentencing outcomes. One reason is that
defendants who finally appear for sentencing are all
members of the low SES classes, due to discrimination
working at the pre-trial or arrest stages, sifting out
the privileged from the system before sentencing.
Another reason is that the distribution of crime in the
population and the risk factors associated with crime
are not associated with discrimination, but perhaps
with social class. Chiricos and Waldo recognize the
limitations of developing SES as a variable. They say:

> Each inmate's socio-economic status was
> measured with techniques developed by
> Nam and Powers, and the U.S. Bureau of
> the Census, which compare the subject's
> income, education, and occupation to
> national distribution of their status
> criteria. Given the backgrounds of
> most persons who filter through the
> criminal justice process to the prison
> level, it makes little sense to speak
> of 'high', middle', 'low' status in tra-
> ditional terms. In fact, 96.6% of the
> offenders in this study had scores
> assigned which were less than 70 on
> a 100-point status scale. Thus, our
> analysis has not attempted to designate
> status groups or levels and the SES
> scores are treated as a continuous
> variable to be correlated with sentences
> received by inmates.[2]

Because of this limitation, this researcher has used
the dichotomous variable, employed or in school,
versus unemployed or out of school, rather than SES
as a variable. Staying in school applies mainly to
youthful offenders under 19 years old. This dichotomous variable would hardly test the conflict theory
because SES includes more than employment versus unemployment. It is difficult to obtain information on SES
for most of the defendants, because verification of in -
come, occupation and education, the three main determinants of SES, is difficult to obtain. Most of the

---

[1]Chiricos and Waldo.

[2]Ibid., 758-9.

defendants are on public assistance or without employment, or in low-level, sporadic jobs, with less than a high school education. Most of them are eligible for legal aid, which has a financial criterion for eligibility. Even those defendants who have a private attorney pay a low fee to these attorneys. This might mean that almost all defendants are members of the low SES class.

However, the variable employment or in school, versus non-employment or out of school, can be important in criminal justice research. Often, defendants who are placed on probation have as a stated condition on their orders of probation the mandatory requirement of seeking job training or employment or remaining in school. Employment is justified as a rehabilitative measure in prognosis in the criminal justice system. A review of the literature reveals that criminal justice actors believe that criminal activity is associated with lack of employment. This reflects some of our society's value systems. Defendants out of work or on welfare might resort to anti-social behavior in order to survive economically or to have the possessions other Americans have.

Staying in school reflects our society's value system also. To become educated is one way, so it is believed, to achieve occupational status and respectability in our society. Judges and probation officers might reflect this value system since they all have college degrees and occupations and incomes indicative of higher-middle class values.

The dichotomous variable employment, in school, versus unemployment, out of school, would hardly test the conflict theory in criminology. However, the variable ethnicity of the offender, the variable ethnicity of the victim, and the offender-victim category are a partial test of the conflict theory, because they involve discrimination. Therefore, this research can be considered as a partial test of the conflict theory.

Organizational Perspective

Many researchers have suggested an organizational perspective in their studies. For example, Eisenstein and Jacob note that although courts don't constitute a bureaucracy, they are organizations. They are not bureaucratic because they lack the hierarchy of bureaucratic organizations. Eisenstein and Jacob perceive

32

the courtroom as a number of workgroups, in which members develop norms and constraints through interaction of the legal actors in an organizational framework.[1]

Mohr notes that organizational analysis doesn't apply to courts. He believes that organizational analysis applies only to the trivial details of the court, such as case assignments, management of some personnel, etc. Mohr notes that a court must have a span of control and a management center to be called an organization; Mohr notes that Weber stated that bureaucracies were characterized by a set of rules, a hierarchy, specialization, span of control and qualifications for office. Mohr notes that courts lack a central management system; there are many management systems. One can question whether there is a set of rules.[2]

Mohr's analysis, however, is debatable.

Hoane in his study of plea bargaining in a New York City criminal court refutes the bureaucratic model of criminal courts. He noted that his court was characterized by public ritual roles, and because of this, couldn't be called a bureaucracy. He noted that Weber had characterized bureaucracies as a hierarchy of offices, strict and systematic discipline, and a contractual method of employment. However, courts use bureaucratic power.

He doubted that courts could be called an organization because of the limited power of the legal actors. He defined the court under study as "a group of officials conducting legal rituals in a partially centralized segmentary system". Following Durkheim, he notes that a segmentary system is composed of similar and similarly functioning parts. According to Hoane, each courtroom has its own role in the system; it is not a bureaucracy. However, it is a system of interrelated parts which is somewhat centralized. Each courtroom is autonomous. The courtroom cannot be integrated into

---

[1]Eisenstein and Jacob, <u>Felony Justice</u>, 9-10.

[2]Laurence B. Mohr, "Organizations, Decisions and Courts", <u>Law and Society Review</u>, Summer, 1976, 10: 624-42.

an organizational machine.[1]

If one assumes an organizational perspective for the courts, one implies that legal actors, such as lawyers, prosecutors, judges and probation officers interact among each other to facilitate the goals of the criminal justice system. Eisenstein and Jacob assume an interaction perspective among legal actors. They say:

> In our view, what judges, prosecutors, defense counsel and others do, depends heavily on how they interact with one another.[2]

They propose the term "workgroups" to define the locus of the interaction in each courtroom. Whether or not courts can be classified as bureaucracies, or even organizations, interaction among legal actors takes place. This researcher assumes that there is interaction between judges and probation officers, among judges, lawyers and prosecutors, between probation officers and lawyers, and between lawyers and prosecutors. This assumption is obtained from the review of the literature and the pilot study to be described in Chapter III.

The influence of legal actors in sentencing dispositions has been studied. Eisenstein and Jacob talk about how judges sentence:

> Our findings conclusively demonstrate the manner in which individual judges are constrained in their sentencing decisions. These constraints also become evident from our observation of the courtroom. Plea negotiations clearly limit the ability of the judge

---

[1]Joseph Hoane, "Stratagems and Values--An Analysis of Plea Bargaining in an Urban Criminal Court", unpublished dissertation for Ph.D., New York University, 1978.

[2]Eisenstein and Jacob, Felony Justice, VI.

himself to affect the sentence
arbitrarily. The courtroom workgroups through their ongoing interactions among major participants
develop norms and expectations about
sentences that constrain all participants in any individual case. No
defendant is sentenced out of con-
text; the sentence he receives be-
comes part of the courtroom's norm.[1]

What Eisenstein and Jacob are implying is that sentencing decisions are shared between the judge and
other actors in the system. Sentencing is not exclusively a judicial function. It is constrained by
norms.

Levine in his study of the courts in Minneapolis
and Pittsburgh states:

More generally in Minneapolis the
sentencing decision is completely
within the purview of the judge and
the prosecutor rarely makes a sentencing recommendation either formally or in open court.[2]

Levine also notes that although judges in Pittsburgh
confer with prosecutors on sentencing, the judge is
still dominant.[3] Here, judges have a great deal of influence in the sentencing decisions. Sentencing is
almost exclusively a judicial function in both cities.

Dawson in his study of three courts in three
cities concluded for one city:

In practice, however, many trial
judges share with others the responsibility for making probation
decisions...When a pre-sentence
report has been prepared, the trial
judges discuss it in chambers, prior

---

[1]Eisenstein and Jacob, _Felony Justice_, 285-6.

[2]Levine, _Urban Politics and Criminal Courts_, 73.

[3]Ibid., 83.

to sentencing with the prosecuting
attorney, and the probation officers,
who prepared the report.[1]

Two of the researchers studied in Chapter I concluded that probation officers share in the sentencing
decisions. Langerman in his study of determinants of
probation officers' recommendations states:

However, this focus on the judge's
role in attempting to understand the
sentencing process, omits the fact
that other agents of influence are
also active in the judicial community
and the social system.[2]

Hagan in his analysis of probation officers' recommendations implicitly addressed this question by proposing
two models in his research, one with and one without
probation officers' recommendations. He found that probation officers' recommendations had a powerful effect
on the sentencing dispositions of judges.[3] Hogarth,
on the other hand, in his study of magistrates in
Canada, found that the probation officer had very
little influence in the sentencing process.[4]

Other actors, such as prosecutors and legal aid
lawyers, also can share in sentencing. James J. Inciardi in a study conducted on 500 cases in Florida for the
year 1974 concluded that prosecutors' recommendations
were very influential in sentencing a defendant to
jail.[5]

---

[1]Robert O. Dawson, Sentencing--the Decision as to
Type, Length, and Conditions of Sentences, Boston:
Little, Brown and Company, 1964, 76, 78.

[2]Langerman, 3.

[3]Hagan, "The Social and Legal Construction of
Criminal Justice--A Survey of Pre-sentence Process,

[4]Hogarth, 373, 376.

[5]James J. Inciardi, "The Impact of Pre-sentence
Procedure on Subsequent Sentencing:, a paper presented
to the 71st Annual Meeting of the American Sociological
Assn., 1976, mimeographed.

This research is modeled after Hagan's study in
Canada because it is a comparative study of judges'
sentencing dispositions both with and without probation
officers' recommendations. This research extends Hagan's
work because it has many more variables than Hagan's
study, and because it uses discriminant analysis in
addition to path analysis to analyze the data. It also
uses interaction terms. It extends Langerman's work
because it includes both the judges' dispositions and
the recommendations of probation officers, as well as
many more crime categories than Langerman used in his study. It
also includes females, youthful offenders, and fines,
which Langerman excluded. This study also includes
promises as a variable. Promises are made by a district attorney as a sentencing recommendation to the
judge. These promises can directly or indirectly
affect sentencing decisions. Since promises are made
in interaction among legal actors, the inclusion of
this variable can help to determine who is influential
in sentencing.

Some of the researchers have concluded that there
is a set of standards or guidelines in sentencing.
Green concludes:

> In summary, the results of this
> investigation contradict the widely
> held notion that there are no stand-
> ards or at best vague ones, by
> which criminal court judges sentence
> convicted defendants...The results
> show a surprising degree of uni-
> formity in sentencing.[1]

Green continues:

> Conversely, in sentencing cases of
> misdemeanors, discretion is con-
> siderably limited due to the rel-
> atively low ceiling on the penal-
> ties authorized by statute, and
> the disposition is apt to be more
> routine.[2]

---

[1]Green, Judicial Attitudes in Sentencing, 48, 71.

[2]Ibid., 19.

Levine in his study of two cities also notes that the judiciary function is constrained by certain factors. Although, for Levine, sentencing is almost exclusively a judicial function, he states:

> Yet the universal complaint that judges are arbitrary and capricious also seems to be inaccurate in Minneapolis and Pittsburgh where their discretionary decisions are highly patterned.[1]

Neubauer, in his study of Prairie City, states:

> An important feature of the sentencing rules in Prairie City is that they are known to all the participants. As with qualifying for probation, the court system in Prairie City operates under a number of well-known but informal rules governing the length of prison term. Participants can predict with a high degree of accuracy who will qualify for probation and who will not.[2]

He continues to say that probation officers' recommendations are routinely accepted.[3] For Neubauer, judges share sentencing decisions with prosecutors, legal aid lawyers, and probation officers.

The term "consistency" is applicable in these discussions. Consistency can be defined as the similar handling of similar cases, or equal sentences for equal cases. If two cases are similar in all factors and one defendant receives jail and the other a conditional discharge, this is an example of inconsistency. Inconsistency implies a different set of standards applicable

---

[1]Levine, Urban Politics and the Criminal Courts, 2-3.

[2]David M. Neubauer, Criminal Justice in Middle America, Morristown: General Learning Press, 1974, 240, 242-3, 249.

[3]Ibid., 97-8.

to similar cases, while consistency implies the same set of standards applicable to similar cases. Some of the researchers discussed consistency in sentencing. Green concluded that if judges were inconsistent, this occurred on cases of intermediate gravity. Cases at the extreme ends of the gravity scale received consistent treatment by judges.[1] Hogarth concluded that judges perceived similar cases in similar ways on cases in which they made decisions, but different judges perceived similar cases differently. In other words, according to Hogarth, judges are consistent within themselves, in their own caseload, but highly inconsistent among themselves.[2]

Many of these regularities and guidelines in sentencing are informal. Many of them are normative. How legal actors acquire these regularities is an empirical quesiton. They can be perceived through the interaction process among legal actors, as in Eisenstein and Jacob's study.[3] These guidelines and regularities structure the sentencing process; they can reduce inconsistency in sentencing and make sentencing decisions a logical, predictable practice.

There is a conflict implied in this discussion. If judges are guided by regularities one can ask if individual attention is given to each defendant in processing his case. Each defendant is different, and different decisions are sometimes required in processing his case. Of course, it is possible for legal actors to be guided by regularities and yet defendants can still receive individual attention. However, the basic conflict still exists because regularities can negate individual attention to each case. On the other hand, if each defendant receives a great amount of individual attention, it is possible for regularities and guidelines to be attenuated.

Imagine the case in which judges are not guided by any set of regularities and they determine each case on the basis of their own perceptions of what is good for the defendant and for society. Any regularities which

---

[1]Green, Judicial Attitudes in Sentencing, 67.

[2]Hogarth, 330.

[3]Eisenstein and Jacob, Felony Justice,

existed in this hypothetical case would be strictly random. Sentencing might be, in this case, capricious, based on the subjective interpretations of the judges. There are goth quantitative and qualitative dimensions to individual attention to cases, and there are both advantages and disadvantages.

Eisenstein and Jacob see no conflict in the above-mentioned argument. They state:

> We do not think courtroom dispositions are assembly line operations. Although many cases flow through courtrooms and most are given little time in any particular day, each receives a remarkable amount of individual attention. As we shall show, one could not substitute a computer for the courtroom as one can for most assembly line operations.[1]

Greenwood and others note that sentencing is not structured by guidelines. In their review of felony cases in Los Angeles, they note:

> These observations merely confirm the fact that defendants convicted fo similar offenses with similar prior records, receive inconsistent treatment in sentencing in the various courts within Los Angeles. No reasonable set of performance standards currently exists for criminal justice agencies.[2]

The researchers do not specify whether or not defendants receive individual attention as a result of inconsistency. Here is an example of inconsistency in spite of certain guidelines, for the researchers note that judges follow probation officers and that

---

[1]Eisenstein and Jacob, Felony Justice, 9.

[2]Peter N. Greenwood, et al., Prosecution of Adult Felony Defendants in Los Angeles County, A Policy Perspective, Santa Monica: Rand Corporation, 1973, 107, 116.

sentencing is consistently more severe with more severe prior records.[1] The consequences of inconsistency are difficult to determine; they can be both positive and negative for the defendant.

Whether or not there are regularities in sentencing, whether or not defendants receive individual attention, consistency among judges and probabion officers, and who is influential in the sentencing process are all topics of research in this book. Whether or not regularities exist and to what extent they exist can partially test an organizational perspective, since organizations do have rules and guidelines for outcomes. Who is influential in sentencing can also partially test an organizational perspective, since organizations do have a hierarchy of influence.

Discretion

The question of regularities and consistency in sentencing involves the concept of discretion. For example, Hogarth states:

> As it is, Canadian law gives enormous
> discretionary power in sentencing to
> magistrates. Magistrates seem to enjoy
> the enormous discretionary power given
> to them and may wish it to be increased.[2]

Kenneth Culp Davis defines discretion:

> A public officer has discretion
> whenever the effective limits on
> his power leave him free to make a
> choice among possible courses of
> action and inaction.[3]

---

[1]Peter N. Greenwood et al., Prosecution of Adult Felony Defendants in Los Angeles County, A Policy Perspective, 24, 39.

[2]Hogarth, 177.

[3]Kenneth Culp Davis, Discretionary Justice--a Preliminary Inquiry, Baton Rouge: Louisiana State University Press, 1969, 4.

However, Davis believes that discretion can have both positive and negative implications. He states:

> Much discretionary justice is without rules--because discretion is preferred to any rules that might be formulated.[1]

Thus, there is a dichotomy between discretion and rules. Davis believes discretion is essential:

> We have not yet found a way to eliminate discretion with respect to arrests, prosecuting, sentencing, paroling and pardoning without destroying crucial values we want to preserve.[2]

Davis recognizes the conflict between regularities and discretion. He asserts:

> Discretionary power can be either too broad or too narrow. When it is too broad, justice may suffer from aribtrariness or inequality. When it is too narrow, justice may suffer from insufficient individualizing.[3]

One can see that consistency, regularities, and individual attention to cases in sentencing are interrelated. If judges and probation officers are too con- sistent, individualization of cases can suffer. If there is too much discretion, there can be too much inequality in sentencing. This study includes research on the relation between consistency, regularities and individual attention to defendants in sentencing. These are three different terms and the relation among terms can vary. For example, judges can be guided by regularities and be either consistent or inconsistent.

---

[1]Kenneth Culp Davis, _Discretionary Justice--a Preliminary Inquiry,_ 5.

[2]Ibid., 18.

[3]Green, _Judicial Attitudes in Sentencing._

Choice of Variables[1]

In this section, the list of variables used in this book will be presented with their symbols. The three-fold classification of variables into legal, relations and personal attributes will be used. In Chapter III the scaling of these variables will be presented.

Legal Variables

1. Number of arrests (NA)[2]

2. Number of convictions (NC)

3. Seriousness of original charge (SOC)

4. Seriousness of final charge (SFC)

5. Seriousness of prior arrests (SPA)

6. Disposition of prior convictions (DPC)

7. Promises (PR)

8. Warrants (WA)

9. Adjustment on prior correctional probram (APP)

10. Pre-trial status (PTS)

11. Recommendations of Probation Officer (RPO)

12. Disposition of judge (DJ)

Most of the legal variables need no explanation. They are the variables found important in reviewing the literature and in the pilot studies conducted by this researcher. Numbers 5 and 6, seriousness of prior arrests and disposition of prior convictions, were used in Green's study in Philadelphia.[3] Number 7, promises,

---

[1]See Table 1 for complete list of variables used in this research.

[2]The letters in parentheses refer to symbols associated with a particular variable.

[3]Green, Judicial Attitudes in Sentencing,

reflects whether or not there was a promise in sentencing by the judge and district attorney, not the actual promise itself. A few studies have indicated that this can have a strong effect in sentencing.[1] It is debatable, however, whether or not this is a legal variable. Number 8, warrants, reflects whether or not a defendant has any warrants, not the actual number of warrants. This can be important in sentencing, although this has appeared virtually not at all in the literature. Number 9, adjustment in prior correctional program, such as probation or parole, can certainly have an effect on sentencing. It is legally required that a defendant adjust favorably on probation and parole. This researcher found this to be important based on the results of the two pilot studies. This variable is hardly mentioned in the review of the literature. The analysis of number 10, pre-trial status, is limited because this can be a study in itself. It is debatable whether number 11, recommendation of probation officer, is or is not a legal variable.

In addition, there are some interaction terms reflecting the legal variables. One or more variables can have weak effects alone, but in interaction they can have very profound effects.

1.   Interaction of recommendations of probation officer, number of arrests and seriousness of final charge.

2.   Interaction of number of convictions and seriousness of final charge.

3.   Interaction of pre-trial status and promises.

4.   Interaction of promises and warrants.

5.   Interaction of adjustment on prior correctional program, number of arrests and seriousness of final charge.

6.   Interaction of final charge and number of arrests.

7.   Interaction of pre-trial status, number of arrests, seriousness of final charge and warrants.

8.   Interaction of number of arrests, seriousness of

---

[1]Inciardi,

final charge and warrants.

Not all of these interaction terms are used in all samples. This researcher sifted out the important ones based on a review of the literature and on the pilot studies.

Personal Attributes

These variables are mostly demographic factors. Many of them are important from a review of the literature.

1. Ethnicity of the defendant (EOD)

2. Ethnicity of the complainant (EOC)

3. Age (AGE)

4. Sex (SEX)

5. Marital Status (MS)

6. Employment Status (ES)

In addition, the following interaction terms are created.

1. Interaction of marital status and employment status.

2. Interaction of ethnicity of defendant and employment.

3. Interaction of ethnicity of the defendant and the number of arrests.

The variables under this classification are important for testing theories of discrimination and social class bias, or the conflict theory.

Relations

The offender-victim categories and legal service are the only two variables used under this classification.

1. Offender-victim category (OV)

2. Legal service (LS)

Variable number 1, offender-victim category, is used to test the theory of discrimination. Variable number 2, type of legal service, was found important in the literature.

Research Questions

In this section, the eight research questions will be posed and defined. These questions are based on the theoretical perspectives developed in Chapters I and II.

1. What factors do judges use in their sentencing dispositions?

2. What factors do probation officers use in their sentencing recommendations?

3. Do judges follow probation officers' recommendations? To what extent?

4. Is there a set of regularities that judges and probation officers follow in their sentencing dispositions and recommendations?

5. Are judges consistent in their sentencing practices?

6. Are probation officers consistent in their sentencing recommendations?

7. Do defendants receive individual attention in the disposition of their cases?

8. Who influences the sentencing process?

Consistency is defined as the handling of similar cases in similar ways. It implies a uniform set of factors in evaluating similar cases; different sets of factors cannot be employed for similar cases. In Chapter IV, a method will be presented to test for "consistency" empirically.

Summary

In this chapter, there were presented some theoretical perspectives on which this research is based. Discrimination, social class bias, organizational theory, and discretion were found applicable to this research. This research can be considered as a partial test of the conflict theory and a partial test of organizational theory. The choice of the variables was based on theoretical perspectives, two pilot studies, and a review of

the literature. This research has included the recommendation of probation officer, seriousness of prior arrests,
disposition of prior convictions, promises, warrants,
adjustment on prior correctional program, as well as
important interaction terms, all of which are not found
very often, or at all, in prior research. The eight
research questions were posed.

The methodology used in this research will be
presented in Chapter III.

Chapter III

METHODOLOGY

In this chapter there will be a discussion of the years from which the samples were drawn, the method of deriving the samples and the sample sizes, the populations from which the samples were derived, and the scaling and coding of the variables. There will be a discussion of one pilot study which involved interviews with judges, prosecutors, legal aid attorneys, and probation officers. There will also be a discussion of a second pilot study which involved a content analyzsis of case records, the results of which were used to develop ideas for this research. As mentioned in Chapter I, this research involved an analysis of both case records from the probation department and court papers from closed files. There will be a discussion of the statistical methods used, namely, path analysis and discriminant analysis, as well as observation.

Years from which Samples are Derived

This research involved an analysis of data for the years 1972, 1973, 1974, the first half of 1975, and the second half of 1976. There was a reason for choosing these particular years. When this researcher started his research in July, 1976, he knew it would be difficult to obtain current probation cases and current court papers from the clerk's office. It would be easier to work on closed cases and closed court papers. On the other hand, this researcher wanted to obtain a significant number of closed probation cases, and therefore he had to go back far enough in years to assure this result. For example, if a defendant were placed on probation for three years in 1972, his case would be closed in 1975, or if he were placed on probation for one year in 1972, his case would be closed in 1973. It is possible for a defendant to be terminated from probation before the maximum expiration date.

The reason why the research had to terminate abruptly in the middle of 1975 was for expediency. The book in the probation department from which the researcher had to gather his sample ended on June 30, 1975. It would have been inadvisable to obtain the books on the population from July 1, 1975 and on, because the clerical staff was working on them at that time. The research resumed for the period April 1, 1976 to December 31, 1976 because of a decision to include cases from pro-forma reports as a third sample, and this is when these reports were used.

Sample Size

There is a logical reason for obtaining a particular sample size; sample size should not be decided upon arbitrarily. Three factors used to determine sample size are now discussed.

Significance Level

Since path analysis was one of the statistical methods used and since path analysis is equivalent to partial correlations, it was necessary to obtain a sample size sufficiently large to obtain significance at a certain level for a certain proportion of variance explained for partial correlations. It is possible to test the significance of a partial correlation by means of an F test. The appropriate formula for testing the significance of path coefficients, or partial correlations, taking into account the number of independent variables, is given by the following F test:

$$F_{1,(n-k-1)} = \frac{r^2 13.2}{1-R^2} \ (n-k-1)$$

where $F_{1,(n-k-1)}$ equals the appropriate degrees of freedom, $r^2 13.2$ equals the partial correlation squared or proportion of variance explained, and $1-R^2$ equals the proportion of variance unexplained. The term $(n-k-1)$ equals the sample size minus the number of independent variables minus one. In practice, however, the partial correlation could include a larger number of variables.[1]

This researcher decided to use 1% for the numerator in the formula for F because any path coefficient

---

[1]Jacob Cohen and Sylvia Cohen, _Applied Multiple Regression/Correlation Analysis for the Behavioral Sciences_, New York: John Wiley & Sons, 1978, 107.

which didn't have a magnitude of at least $\pm$ .10 was eliminated from the analysis. He also decided to use the .05 level of significance, although this can be arbitrary. There is a debate in the literature for choosing the significance level in tests of significance.[1] This researcher believed that a .01 significance level might be too stringent. One can solve the appropriate F test by solving for n, or sample size, with a critical value of alpha and F, and adjust for missing cases. This researcher wanted to be over-cautious and decided on a safe figure for K, or number of independent variables of about 30. The final sample size for sample 1 and 2 was estimated at about 1000 each, and for sample 3 at about 100 cases. This would certainly meet significance for samples 1 and 2 and to a more limited extent for sample 3.

Power Analysis

Generally speaking, the larger the sample on which the population is based, the more confidence one has that the sample represents the population under study. However, other considerations limit the choice of sample size, such as expediency, access to sample, time limitations, costs, etc. One factor is the concept of power. Power is defined on the basis of a distribution between two types of erroneous inference. A type I error is the rejection of the null hypothesis when it is true. A Type II error is the failure to reject the null hypothesis when it is false. Power of a test is defined as one minus the probability of rejecting the null hypothesis when it is true, the probability that the research will result in the conclusion that the phenomenon exists.

As Cohen and Cohen point out, the power of a test depends on the alpha or significance level, the sample size, the number of independent variables, and the effect size. Cohen and Cohen define the effect size as the degree to which the phenomenon exists, the degree to which the null hypothesis is false. Cohen and Cohen state that power depends on whether or not one uses a two-tail or one-tail test. A two-tail test of

---

[1]Denton E. Morrison and R. E. Hankel, The Significance Test Controversy--a Reader, Chicago: Aldine, 1970.

51

a certain alpha will have less power than a one-tail test of the same significance level.

Cohen and Cohen give the formulas for the power of a test and for the appropriate sample size when certain parameters are known. The formula for the power of the test is:

$$L = f^2 (n-k-1)$$

where L = appropriate power level

f^2 = effect size

n = sample size

k = number of independent variables

The formula for the sample size is:

$$n = \frac{L}{f^2} + k + 1$$

where the terms are the same as in the formula for L. There are four unknowns in each equation; if one knows three of the four parameters, the fourth one is determined by solving the appropriate equations.

Cohen and Cohen give three effect sizes, small, which is equivlent to .02, medium, which is equal to .15, and large, which is equal to .35. They recommend a power level of .80 and effect size of .15, but they talk about lower power levels.[1]

This researcher was uncertain initially of the number of variables to be used in the research. Variables were added and deleted during the research stages. One can take an overestimate to be cautious. It turned out that sample 1 consisted of 983 cases and 40 independent variables, sample 2 consisted of 836 cases and 31 independent variables, and sample 3 consisted of 100 cases and 16 independent variables. Solving the

---

[1]Cohen and Cohen, Applied Multiple Regression Correlation Analysis for the Behavioral Sciences, 9-10, 54,56, 131-2, 152, and Jacob Cohen, Statistical Power Analysis for the Behavioral Sciences, New York: Academic Press, 1969.

equation for L or power and looking at an appropriate
table provided by Cohen, it turned out that with an
effect size of .02, there was between .60 and .70 power
for sample 1, between .50 and .60 power for sample 2,
and between .70 and .75 power for sample 3. With an
effect size of .15, power would be increased. One must
sacrifice sample size, effect size, number of independent variables, or alpha for power. The F test is only
a one-tail test, so power is not being sacrificed
here.[1] The numerator of the F test is really the
effect size which Cohen and Cohen talk about. It
turned out that many variables were deleted from the
first stages of path analysis thus increasing the
power of the test. This researcher believes that he
has a minmum of .50 power and a maximum of .75 for the
samples as a conservative estimate, but there is
probably greater power for the samples at later stages
of the analysis.

Confidence Intervals

One can look at this from another point of view.
One can transform the r, or partial correlation, into
a Z statistic, which has a sampling distribution which
is approximately normal, and place confidence intervals
around the Z statistic. The Z values are then
reconverted into r's, and confidence limits are
obtained for r's. The formula for the standard error
of a Z statistic is:

$$S.D._Z = \frac{1}{\sqrt{N-k-2}}$$

where N is the sample size, and k is the number of
independent variables. Since this research involves 983
cases in sample 1 and 40 independent variables, 836
cases in sample 2 and 31 independent variables, and 100
cases in sample 3 and 16 independent variables, the
appropriate standard errors of the Z statistic are .03
for samples 1 and 2, and .11 for sample 3. One can
place a 95% confidence interval around the Z statistic.
The appropriate Z statistic for r = .10 = z = .10.

---

[1]Hubert M. Blalock, Jr., Social Statistics, Second
Edition, New York: McGraw Hill, 1972, 325.

Therefore, the confidence levels for Z in samples 1 and 2 are Z = .10 $\pm$ 1.96 (.03) = .10 $\pm$ .06 = .16, .04. The r values corresponding to the Z values are .159 and .04.

In other words, one can be 95% confident that the partials or path coefficients range from .04 to .159. For sample 3, the confidence levels for Z are Z=.10 $\pm$ 1.96 (.11) = .10 $\pm$ .22 = .32, -.12. In other words, one can be 95% confident that the path coefficients range from -.12 to .31. Appropriate confidence intervals can be placed around higher-value coefficients.

The appropriate sample size for path analysis is also appropriate for discriminant analysis. Discriminant analysis is an appropriate method for deriving discriminant functions. The canonical correlation, which is defined as an association between a group and a discriminant function, is equivalent when squared, to the eta in one-way analysis of variance. The appropriate discriminant function coefficients are analogous in interpretation to beta weights in multiple regression.[1]

Population

There are three samples and three different models. The models will be discussed further in this chapter. Sample 1 consists of a systematic sample of cases in which judges sentence with a probation report. Sample 2 consists of a systematic sample of cases in which judges sentence without a probation report. Sample 3 consists of a systematic sample of cases from pro-forma reports. The pro-forma reports are short reports written by the probation officers without verification of the factors or without a recommendation. The defendants are practically all in remand and usually, but not always, receive prison as a disposition.

The sampling frame for sample 1 was obtained from books in the probation department which listed

---

[1] Norman H. Nie, et. al., _Statistical Package for the Social Sciences_, New York: McGraw Hill, 1975, 442-443.

information on cases processed from January 1, 1972
through June 30, 1975. This researcher obtained a
systematic sample of 1021 cases from a population of
approximately 17,000 cases for sample 1. After eliminating cases with missing items and those convicted
after trial, sample 1 consisted of 983 cases.

For sample 2, the researcher drew a systematic
sample for each of the 20 judges who had the most cases
in sample 1 for the years 1972 through June, 1975. The
sampling frame for sample 2 was obtained from adjournment books located in the clerk's office. These were
all cases in which a sentence was made without a probation report. In order to obtain a systematic sample
for each of the 20 judges in sample 2, the population
of sentencing dispositions for each judge for the
years 1972 through June, 1975 had to be composed. This
counting proces involved several months of work. One
judge had to be eliminated because of inaccessibility
to closed court papers, reducing the total number of
judges to 19. The mean number of cases per judges was
44. Sample 3 was obtained easily from books in the
probation department from a total population of 400.

This researcher checked the books from which the
samples were drawn and found that there was no evidence
of a trend or a cyclical characteristic in the data.
This can cause biases in the data, and a systematic
sample will not be equivalent to a simple random
sample.[1]

This researcher was refused access to active
probation cases, but he doesn't believe that a bias
occurred because there was no reason to believe that
there was a difference between active and closed
probation cases.

The researcher did not attempt to obtain an equal
number of cases for each year, but every year is
represented in each sample. This researcher tried to
get information from the probation department and from
the statistics department. The probation department
had no available statistics, and the statistics
department had the total number of dispositions by year

---

[1]Blalock, 515.

and by part, but these were not broken down by judge or by disposition. A review of the literature reveals that courts usually don't keep up-to-date statistics. However, in spite of these limitations, this researcher believes that he has obtained true probability samples for all cases because he has designed his research that way, adhering strictly to the rules of sampling.

Pilot Study One

In one pilot study, this researcher conducted interviews with 12 legal aid attorneys, 10 district attorneys, 9 judges, 7 probation officers, and a separate interview with 20 probation officers. All of these legal actors worked at Brooklyn Criminal Court. The judges interviewed were the same ones who appeared in the three samples. Some, but not all of the probation officers interviewed, were the same ones who appeared in the sample. The other legal actors were not necessarily the same ones in the original samples, since there is a great deal of turnover among legal aid lawyers and prosecutors.

The purpose of the interviews with the 20 probation officers was to ascertain the scaling of the seriousness of present and past charges. The probation officers generally agreed on the three-fold classification of crimes against persons, crimes against property, and victimless crimes, with crimes against persons the most serious and victimless crimes the least serious. There were two exceptions to this classification. Possession of a weapon and possession of drugs, although victimless crimes, were considered to be midway between crimes against the person and victimless crimes, and they were classified in the middle range of seriousness of charge.

The interviews with the legal actors revealed that they generally used the same variables or factors in their sentencing dispositions and recommendations as the ones reported in the review of the literature. Seriousness of charge and prior record seem to be most important for district attorneys' recommendation and judges' disposition, both in sentencing and in pre-trial status. The personal characteristics and community ties of the defendant are very important. Employment is also very important. The district attorneys make either a promise or a recommendation in many cases which involves negotiations among judges, district attorneys, and lawyers. These promises or recommendations also pertain to pre-trial status. The judges are obliged to follow these promises or recommendations.

56

Pilot Study Two

In a second pilot study, the researcher has analyzed the reasons given by probation officers for a particular recommendation. Usually the probation officer writes a one- or two-paragraph statement in the case record on why he recommends a particular disposition, and this researcher has analyzed every case for content of the reasons. Although probation officers give reasons, these can be rationalizations, rather than true reasons, in order to impress the supervisor, branch chief, or judge. This is why the researcher decided to analyze these reasons in a pilot study for ideas for research rather than as findings. A count of all the reasons was made for all cases in sample 1, and the reasons were classified into categories.

The number of arrests and convictions was mentioned as the most frequent reason for a recommendation. The fact that the defendant was under a particular agency, e.g., probation or drug facility, was mentioned second, and treatment and rehabilitation was mentioned third. The fourth most frequent reason was adjustment on prior correctional program, e.g., probation or parole. The least frequent reasons were pre-trial status, marital status, and warrants. Employment status and nature of the offense were in the mid-frequency ranges.

Many, but not all, of the reasons were used as variables in the research. The number of arrests and convictions and adjustment on prior correctional programs were used as variables in the research. Pre-trial status, employment status, number of warrants, and marital status were used as variables in the research. It was preferable to use some of the most frequent and least frequent reasons cited by probation officers. Treatment and rehabilitation was not used as a variable because it was defined ambiguously in the case records.

Some excerpts from the probation reports on reasons for particular dispositions can illustrate the idea:

> We are recommending this man be given a conditional discharge.

57

> The incident appears isolated and
> he is apparently making satisfactory
> progress in his probationary period.
> Conditional discharge--cooperate with
> term of your Supreme Court probation.

Here, two variables are isolated, adjustment on prior
correctional program and number of arrests, e.g., good
adjustment in Supreme Court, and no prior record.

Another probation officer records:

> We feel that the present offense is
> serious; also, the defendant isn't
> working which might add to his
> problem. We feel supervision is
> indicated and we recommend probation
> for the instant offense.

Here, two variables are isolated, seriousness of
charge and employment status.

Scaling of the Variables

In this section, there will be a discussion of
the scaling and coding of variables. Most of the
variables used in this research are on an ordinal or
nominal level of measurement rather than on an interval level of measurement. However, a review of the
literature reveals that measurement on the ordinal
level meets the requirement of interval data in path
analysis.[1] A review of the literature also reveals
that discriminant analysis is sensitive to ordinal
data used as interval data,[2] but most of the
variables used in this research are coded as dummy
variables, thus avoiding this problem.

---

[1]Richard F. Boyle, "Path Analysis and Ordinal
Data," American Journal of Sociology, January, 1970,
461-80.

[2]Donald G. Morrison, "Discriminant Analysis," in
Robert Ferber, Handbook of Marketing Research, New
York: McGraw-Hill, 1974.

Most of the variables are coded as dummy variables. Each category of a nominal variable coded as a dummy variable is treated as a separate category. Dummy variables can be analyzed in the same fashion as interval data.[1] No assumptions need to be made about linearity, and additivity is assumed.[2]

The following is a complete list of the variables used in this research as well as a discussion of the method used to scale and code the variables.

The following is the list of dummy variables:

1. Ethnicity of the defendant (EOD)[3]

   a. X_1, Y_1, Z_1[4] = Dummy variable for ethnicity of the defendant, coded 1 for White, 0 otherwise.

   b. X_2, Y_2, Z_2 = Dummy variable for ethnicity of the defendant, coded 1 for Black, 0 otherwise.

   c. Y_3 = Dummy variable for ethnicity of the defendant, coded 1 for Puerto Rican, 0 otherwise.[5]

2. Age of the defendant (AGE)

   a. X_3, Y_4, Z_3 = Dummy variable for age, coded 1 for age under 19, 0 otherwise.

---

[1]Boyle.

[2]John A. Sonquist, Multivariate Model Building, Ann Arbor: University of Michigan Press, 1970, 11.

[3]Letters in parentheses are the symbols used for the variables. See Table 1 for a complete list of variables.

[4]Variables designated X are from sample 1, variables designated Y are from sample 2, and those designated z from sample 3.

[5]Some categories of nominal variables had to be classified as "not known" due to the danger of loss of hundreds of cases through "listwise deletion" of the computer program.

This classification into under 19, and 19 and over is logical, because youthful offender status is usually but not always granted to offenders who commit crimes between 16 and before the 19th birthday. A youthful offender has a record of arrest, but not of conviction, and there is no public record of his crime; his record is sealed.

3. Sex of the defendant (SEX)

   a. X4, Y5, Z4 = Dummy variable for sex, coded 1 for male, 0 otherwise.

4. Marital Status of the defendant (MS)

   a. X5, Y6 = Dummy variable for marital status, coded 1 for married, either legally or common-law, 0 otherwise.

   b. Y7 = Dummy variable for marital status, coded 1 for unmarried, single, divorced, widow, widower, 0 otherwise.

5. Employment status of the defendant (ES)

   a. X6, Y8 = Dummy variable for employment status, coded 1 for employed, in school, 0 otherwise.

   b. Y9 = Dummy variable for employment status, coded 1 for unemployed, out of school, 0 otherwise.

6. Promises recorded on court papers (PR)

   a. X7, Z5 = Dummy variable for promises, coded 1 for promises, 0 otherwise.

   b. X8 = Dummy variable for promises, coded 1 for no promises, 0 otherwise.

7. Warrants recorded in probation records or court papers (WA)

   a. X9, Y10, Z6 = Dummy variable for warrants, coded 1 for 1 or more warrants, 0 otherwise.

   b. X10 = Dummy variable for warrants, coded 1 for no warrants, 0 otherwise.

8. Adjustment on prior correctional program (APP)

a. X11 = Dummy variable for adjustment, coded 1 for poor adjustment, 0 otherwise.

b. X12 = Dummy variable for adjustment, coded 1 for good adjustment, 0 otherwise.

9. Ethnicity of the complainant (EOC)

   a. X13, Y11, Z7 = Dummy variable for ethnicity of the complainant, coded 1 for White, 0 otherwise.

   b. X14, Y12, Z8 = Dummy variable for ethnicity of the complainant, coded 1 for Black, 0 otherwise.

   c. X15, Y13, Z9 = Dummy variable for ethnicity of the complainant, coded 1 for Puerto Rican, 0 otherwise.

10. Offender-victim category

    a. X16, Y14, Z10 = Dummy variable for offender-victim category, coded 1 for White vs. White, government, 0 otherwise.

    b. X17, Y15 = Dummy variable for offender-victim category, coded 1 for White vs. Black, Puerto Rican, 0 otherwise.

    c. X18, Y16, Z11 = Dummy variable for offender-victim category, coded 1 for Black, Puerto Rican vs. White, government, 0 otherwise.

    d. X19, Y17, Z12 = Dummy variable for offender-victim category, coded 1 for Black, Puerto Rican vs. Black, Puerto Rican, 0 otherwise.

11. Pre-trial status (PTS)

    a. X20, Y21 = Dummy variable for pre-trial status, coded 1 for remand, 0 otherwise.

    b. Y22 = Dummy variable for pre-trial status, coded 1 for out of remand, 0 otherwise.

12. Type of legal service (LS)

    a. X21, Y18 = Dummy variable for legal service, coded 1 for legal aid, 0 otherwise.

61

b. Y19 = Dummy variable for legal service, coded 1 for legal aid and private lawyer, 0 otherwise.

c. Y20 = Dummy variable for legal service, coded 1 for private lawyer, 0 otherwise.

The following interaction terms are coded both as dummy variables and scaled on interval levels of measurement.

13. X22 = Interaction of recommendation of probation officer, number of arrests, seriousness of final charge, (RPO) (NA) (SFC).

14. X23 = Interaction of number of convictions, seriousness of final charge, (NC) (SFC).

15. X24 = Interaction of remand and promises, (X20) (X7).

16. X25 = Interaction of employment status and marital status, (X5) (X6).

17. X26 = Interaction of warrants and promises, (X7) (X9).

18. X27 = Interaction of White complainant and the offender-victim category of Black, Puerto Rican defendant vs. White complainant, government agency, (X13) (X18).

19. X28 = Interaction of poor adjustment in a prior correctional program, number of arrests, seriousness of final charge, (X11) (NA) (SFC).

20. X29 = Interaction of good adjustment in a prior correctional program, number of arrests, seriousness of final charge, (X12) (NA) (SFC).

21. X30 = Interaction of White defendant and employment, (X1) (X6).

22. Interaction of Black defendant and employment, (X2) (X6).

23. X32 = Interaction of White defendant and number of arrests, (X1) (NA).

24. X33 = Interaction of Black defendant and number of arrests, (X2) (NA).

25. Y23 = Interaction of number of arrests and seriousness of final charge, (NA) (SFC).

26. Y24 = Interaction of remand, number of arrests, seriousness of final charge, warrants, (Y21) (NA) (SFC) (Y10).

27. Y25 = Interaction of number of arrests, seriousness of final charge, warrants, (NA) (SFC) (Y10).

The following variables are either interval scales or ordinal data scaled on interval levels of measurement.

28. Seriousness of original charge (SOC)

This is an ordinal scale but an interval level of measurement is assumed. This variable is coded according to the threefold classification of crimes against persons, crimes against property, and victimless crimes, with crimes against persons considered the most serious and victimless crimes the least serious, and crimes against property in-between. As mentioned earlier, interviews with probation officers substantiated this classification with two exceptions, namely, possession of a weapon and possession of drugs, which were put into the middle-range of seriousness of original charge. Very often, the placement of a charge into a given category is subjective and requires a judgment. Criminal tresspassing, for example, was placed in the middle range of seriousness. In the event of multiple charges, the first charge recorded in the case record was used.

This variable is coded 1 for crimes against persons, 2 for crimes against property, or possession of drugs, or possession of a weapon, and 3 for victimless crimes.

29. Seriousness of final charge (SFC)

This is coded and scaled in the same way as seriousness of original charge.

30. Number of arrests (NA)

This is measured on an interval scale and is the

actual number of arrests, including zero arrests, but excluding the present or instant charge.

31. Number of convictions (NC)

This is measured on an interval scale and is the actual number of convictions including zero convictions, but excluding the present or instant charge.

32. Seriousness of prior arrests (SPA)

This is an ordinal scale, but an interval level of measurement is assumed. This variable is coded initially in the same way as seriousness of original and final charge, in which crimes against persons are coded 1, crimes against property or possession of drugs, or possession of a weapon are coded 2, victimless crimes are coded 3, and no prior record is coded 4. Crimes against persons are the most serious category, and no prior record is the least serious category.

It was impossible due to time limitations for this researcher to investigate every arrest. Sometimes probation officers verify every arrest and sometimes they don't. Therefore, this researcher coded each prior arrest that fell into a new category, summed the categories, and divided by the number of categories. For example, if a defendant had 10 prior arrests, 5 for assault, and 5 for petit larceny, his SPA score would be

$$\frac{1 + 2}{2} = 1.5.$$

Here, assault falls into category 1, crimes against persons, and petit larceny falls into category 2, crimes against property. This was done for sample 1 only. For samples 2 and 3, each arrest was coded separately and SPA scores were obtained by dividing the summation of categories by the number of arrests instead of by the number of categories. This researcher found the results of the two methods very similar. In the event of multiple charges, the most serious one was recorded. Sometimes the original charge was used and sometimes the final charge was used.

33. Disposition of prior convictions (DPC)

This variable is an ordinal scale but an interval level of measurement is assumed, from the most severe disposition to the least severe disposition. For this variable, jail, or commitment to a drug facility as an in-patient, or time served, the most serious category, is coded 1, probation of a split sentence[1] is coded 2, conditional or unconditional discharge, or fine, is coded 3, and no prior convictions, the less severe category, is coded 4.

For sample 1, this researcher wasn't able to look up every prior disposition because of time limitations; therefore, he coded each disposition that fell into a new category, summed the categories, and divided by the number of categories. For example, if an offender received jail 3 times, probation 2 times, and fine 1 time, his DPC score

$$= \frac{1 + 2 + 3}{3} = 2.$$

In sample 2, this researcher coded each disposition separately, and the DPC score was obtained by summing the total number of prior disposition categories for each arrest and dividing by the number of arrests. This researcher found little difference in the results between both methods used in samples 1 and 2.

34. Recommendation of probation officer (RPO)

This is the actual sentencing recommendation of the probation officer which was recorded in the case record. This is an ordinal scale, but an interval level of measurement is assumed, from the most severe to the least severe recommendation. Jail, or commitment to a drug facility as an in-patient, or time served, the most severe recommendation is coded 1, probation or split sentence is coded 2, conditional discharge is coded 3, fine is coded 4, and unconditional discharge, the least severe recommendation, is coded 5.

35. Disposition of the judge (DJ)

---

[1] A split sentence is a maximum period of 60 days jail and the remainder of time on probation.

This variable is an ordinal scale but it is scaled on an interval level of measurement from the most severe disposition to the least severe disposition. Jail, or commitment to a drug facility as an inpatient, or time served, the most severe disposition is coded 1, probation or split sentence is coded 2, conditional discharge is coded 3, fine is coded 4, and unconditional discharge, the least severe disposition, is coded 5.

In addition, each probation officer and judge in the research was assigned a number which had no relation to his or her name. This number was used strictly by the researcher for identification purposes to aid in the analysis. This numbering system was quite arbitrary.

Quantitative Analysis

As mentioned in Chapter 1, path analysis and discriminant analysis are used in this research to analyze the data. With some exceptions, many of the researchers, especially before 1960, mainly used non-parametric methods, such as chi-square, to analyze their data. This is inappropriate for sentencing studies today, because there are too many variables used in research and non-parametric methods are difficult to carry out with more than one or two variables. Multivariate methods based on the general linear model are potentially more informative than non-parametric methods.

Path Analysis

Three models are proposed for path analysis. Three samples are drawn from three different populations, namely, a population in which probation officers make a recommendation, a population in which judges sentence without a probation recommendation, and a population of pro-forma reports, in which a probation officer makes a short report without a recommendation. The design of the three models is given in Tables 2, 3 and 4. These tables show the direction of causality, and the complete list of variables used initially in the analysis. These are full models, with all variables except multicollinear variables, high correlations between independent varia-

66

bles,[1] which will be discussed in Chapter IV, and with the exclusion of variables due to theoretical limitations.

Table 2

Path Analysis--Full Model 1[a]

Effects	Pre-trial Status(PTS)[b]	Dependent Variable Recom. of Prob. Off.(RPO)	Disposition of Judge
Direct	X1 to X12, X15,X17 to X19,X21,X26 X28 to X31, SFC,NA,SPA,DPC	X1 to X12, X15,X17 to X21,X24,X26 X28 to X31, SFC,NA,SPA,DPC	X1 to X12, X15,X17 to X21,X24,X26, X28 to X31, SFC,NA,SPA,DPC, RPO
Indirect	All variables indirectly affecting PTS	All variables indirectly affecting RPO	All variables indirectly affecting DJ
Total	Direct + indirect effects	Direct + indirect effects	Direct + indirect effects

[a]This researcher decided to use tables instead of path diagrams for all path analyses because of the complications involved in devising path diagrams for a large number of variables.

[b]See Table 1 for a complete list of variables.

Model 1 is the one with the probation recommendation. It was found in Chapter I that the recommendation of probation officer was very important in several studies.

[1]See appendices A, B, and C for a complete list of zero order correlations. In this research, the cut-off point for multicollinearity is $\pm$ .70 or above.

Table 3

Path Analysis--Full Model 2[a]

Effects	Remand (Y21)	Dependent Variable: Out of Remand (Y22)	Disposition of Judge
Direct	Yl to Y10, Y13 to Y20, Y25,SOC,SFC, NA,SPA,DPC	Yl to Y10, Y13 to Y20, Y25,SOC,SFC, NA,SPA,DPC	Yl to Y10, Y13 to Y22 Y24,Y24,Y25, SOC,SFC,NA, SPA,DPC
Indirect	All variables indirectly affecting Y21	All variables indirectly affecting Y22	All variables indirectly affecting DJ
Total	Direct plus indirect effects	Direct plus indirect effects	Direct plus indirect effects

[a]See Table 1 for a complete list of variables.

In Model 1, there are three dependent variables, pre-trial status, recommendation of probation officer, and disposition of judge. The variables X13, X14, X16, X22, X23, X25, X27 X32, X33, SOC and NC have been eliminated due to multicollinearity.

With pre-trial status as the dependent variable, all the multicollinear terms plus X20 and X24 have been eliminated because these latter two variables measure pre-trial status directly or indirectly. With RPO, rec-ommendation of probation officer as dependent variable, all the multicollinear variables plus RPO have been elimi-nated from the full model. With disposition of judge as dependent variable, all the multicollinear variables have been eliminated. However, RPO is included. One can see by looking at Table 2 that all the independent variables di-rectly affect the three dependent variables. The indirect effects are obtained by subtracting the direct effects from th

Table 4

Path Analysis--Full Model 3[a]

Effects	Dependent Variable Disposition of Judge (DJ)
Direct	Z2 to Z6, Z8, Z9, Z11, SOC, SFC, NA, SPA
Indirect	All variables indirectly affecting DJ
Total	Direct effects plus indirect effects

[a]See Table 1 for a complete list of variables

zero order correlations of the two variables in question. Total effects are obtained by adding direct and indirect effects.

Model 2 is the one without the recommendations of the probation officers. A comparison of dispositions of judges between a model with and without probation officers' recommendations is important because this can tell how much weight the probation officer's recommendation has in the sentencing process. It can also tell the relative amount of influence the probation officer has in sentencing. A model without a probation officer's recommendation can show how judges sentence when they are not aided by the probation officer.

In Model 2, Y11, Y12, Y23 and NC are eliminated because of multicollinearity. There are three dependent variables. The dependent variables, Y21, Y22, and pre-trial status, have every variable affecting them directly except the four multicollinear variables and Y21, Y22, and Y24, because these latter variables measure pre-trial status. Here, every variable directly affects pre-trial status. With disposition of judge as dependent variable, all variables are included except the multicollinear variables and every variable directly affects the dependent variable.

Just as in Model 1, the indirect effects are

69

obtained by subtracting the direct effects from the zero-order correlations of the two variables in question. The total effects are obtained by adding the direct and the indirect effects.

In Model 3, there is only one dependent variable, disposition of judge. This is the model which consists of pro-forma reports in which probation officers write a short report, without verifying the facts or making a sentencing recommendation. Practically all the defendants are in remand; therefore, pre-trial status is not one of the variables used in this model. In this model, the multicollinear variables Z7 and Z12 are eliminated. In addition, Z1 and Z10 are excluded because there are few cases in these categoreis. Here, every variable directly affects the dependent variable. The indirect effects and total effects are obtained in the same way as in Models 1 and 2.

Models 1 and 2 are shown in Figures 1 and 2. It can be seen that in Model 1, both legal and extra-legal variables affect X20, pre-trial status, RPO, recommendation of probation officer, and DJ, disposition of the judge directly, and RPO and DJ indirectly. Pre-trial status, X20, directly affects RPO and DJ, and indirectly affects DJ, and RPO directly affects DJ. The variables X20, and RPO are both dependent and independent variables. In Model 2, the legal and extra-legal variables directly affect Y21, remand, and Y22, out of remand, and both directly and indirectly affect DJ. The variables Y21 and Y22 are both dependent and independent variables. In Model 3, there is only one dependent variable, DJ, disposition of the judge, and thus the statistical methods are like regression analysis.

These are only three possible models. Other models are possible. For example, it is possible to let NA, number of arrests, intervene between the legal and extra-legal variables and the dependent variables in Models 1 and 2. It is possible that number of arrests can be influenced by ethnicity of the defendant, employment, marital status, age, etc. However, the zero-order correlations between NA and the other variables are rather low (see Appendices A, B, and C). This researcher doesn't believe that assuming a model in which NA is another dependent variable would change the results of the path coefficients very much. In addition, the number of arrests as a dependent varia-

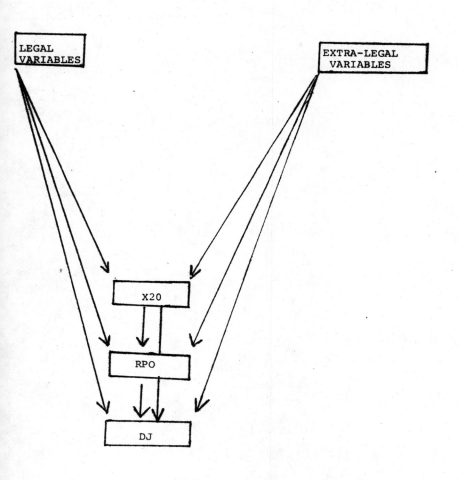

Fig. 1.   Path Analysis--Model 1.

71

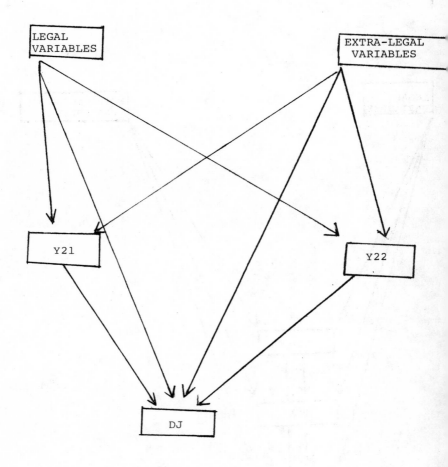

Fig. 2.   Path Analysis--Model 2.

72

ble can be a study in itself, since there are many factors which influence the arrest rate, such as suspects' demeanors, personality of the arresting officer, the social and economic conditions of the community in which the crime was committed, etc. This researcher believes that pre-trial status, recommendation of the probation officer, and disposition of the judge are the three main areas of the sentencing decisions.

The reduced models are more parsimonious models compared to the full models. In the reduced models, paths which neither obtain a magnitude of $\pm$ .10 or above nor are significant on at least a .05 level are eliminated from further analysis. Both criteria must be met. However, these two criteria are not independent of each other; they both depend on the sample size. Generally, paths which fail to meet one criterion also fail to meet the other criterion, but there are some paths which meet one criterion but fail to meet the other criterion.

Here, the recursive model is used. This assumes that the direction of the effect of the independent variables to the dependent variable is one way; there is no two-way feedback between independent variables to dependent variable and from dependent variable to independent variables. In the recursive model, the researcher is always assured of having a completely identified system. This enables the path coefficients to be solved by a set of simultaneous equations.

Path coefficients can be either standardized or unstandardized. A review of the literature reveals that if one is interested in comparing one variable to another in the same population, the standardized path coefficients are preferable. If one is interested in comparing one population to another, or in observing causal laws or processes, the unstandardized path coefficients are preferable.[1] However, the choice is really made on theoretical grounds. In this research, both standardized and unstandardized path coefficients will be presented. The standardized path coefficients will be used to show the proportion of variance explained for each variable in each sample, and the

---

[1]Nie et al., 396-7.

unstandardized path coefficients will be used to show the unit change in the dependent variable due to a unit change in the independent variable.

Discriminant Analysis

Discriminant analysis is a procedure which separates two or more groups on the basis of discriminant functions which consist of a linear combination of discriminating variables. Technically, "the linear function of the X variable which maximizes the ratio of the between means of groups sum of squares to within groups sum of squares has been named the discriminant function."[1] Tatsuoka defines it as "this approach of constructing a linear combination, thus reducing the problem of group differences to a univariate problem (or, even if multivariate, one which usually involves far fewer variables than the original set) is known as discriminant analysis."[2] The discriminant functions are obtained by means of varying statistics, including minimum between groups F, largest increase in average multiple correlation and largest increase in Rao's V.[3]

The maximum number of discriminant functions is either the number of groups minus one or is equal to the number of variables, whichever is smaller. In this research, the recommendation of the probation officer and the disposition of the judge are the two variables defined as the groups for discriminant analysis. Therefore, since there are five groups for both recommendation of the probation officer and disposition of judge in sample 1, corresponding to the five different sentencing dispositions, it is possible to have four functions each for both variables in sample 1. Likewise it is possible to have three functions in sample 2 for disposition of judge, since there are only four sentencing dispositions in sample 2. In

---

[3]Nie et al., 434.

[1]Joseph G. Bryan, "The Generalized Discriminant Function--Mathematical Foundation and Computational Routine," Harvard Educational Review, 1951, 21:90-95.

[2]Maurice M. Tatsuoka, Discriminant Analysis: The Study of Group Differences, Champaign: Institute for Personality and ABility Testing, 1970, 4-5.

74

sample 3, there are only three groups, so it is possible to have two functions for disposition of judge. Pre-trial status will not be analyzed in samples 1 and 2, since this is coded as a dichotomy, and nothing new could be learned by analyzing this variable.

There are ways of checking the relative contribution of each discriminant function. The eigenvalue tells us the relative importance of each function. The sum of the eigenvalues is a measure of the total variance existing in the discriminating variables. The canonical correlation is a measure of correlation between discriminant functions and the groups. The canonical correlation squared is the proportion of variance in the discriminant function explained by the group.[1]

Discriminant analysis is a way of classifying cases from the sample, and by measuring the differences between the predicted and observed group membership, one can derive the success of discriminant functions in classifying the cases.[2] The difference between the predicted and observed group membership can be easily converted into a value which is analogous to R^2 in regression. The classification equations are derived from the pooled within group covariance matrix and from the centroids or group means.[3]

More will be said about discriminant functions in Chapter IV, where the functions will be plotted. More will be said about the eigenvalues and the canonical correlations.

The coefficients of the discriminant functions are analogous to beta weights or path coefficients in path analysis. All functions can be named on the basis of variables which have the highest values, either positive or negative. In other words, a function is named on the basis of its most discriminating

---

[1] Ibid., 442.

[2] Ibid., 445.

[3] Ibid.

variables. Variables which either don't meet a certain statistical criterion or are multicollinear are eliminated from the analysis.

All statistical computations for this research were obtained from the computers of New York University's computer center, and the language employed was SPSS.

Observation

As mentioned in Chapter 1, this researcher was a probation officer at Brooklyn Criminal Court since March 1, 1972. Therefore, he acted as an observer and participant observer of events in the courts. Trained in sociology, this researcher tried to use the scientific method in observing and forming conclusions about the sentencing recommendations and practices of probation officers and judges. Since quantitative analysis is the principal method used in this research, observation will be limited to a very small part of this research, mostly used to verify the findings of the quantitative analysis.

Summary

The methodology used in this research was discussed in this chapter. The final sample size of 983 cases for sample 1, 836 cases for sample 2, and 100 cases for sample 3 were of sufficient size to meet criteria for significance, power, and confidence levels, three factors used in determining sample size. Path analysis and discriminant analysis were the statistical methods used to analyze the data. Three models were proposed, and three samples were drawn. Model 1 included the recommendation of probation officer, Model 2 excluded the recommendation of probation officer, and Model 3 was based on pro-forma reports, short reports written by probation officers with neither verification of the facts nor a recommendation.

The full models included all variables except either multicollinear variables, variables with high correlations between independent variables, or variables excluded on the basis of theoretical perspectives. The reduced models not only excluded multicollinear variables, but also certain paths which didn't meet certain criteria. In path analysis, path coefficients which neither had a magnitude of ± .10 or above nor were significant on at least the .05 level, were eliminated from later stages of the analysis. As

a result, the reduced models consist of fewer paths
compared to the full models. Variables which didn't
meet certain criteria for significance and multicollinear variables were eliminated from discriminant
analysis.

The scaling and coding of the variables were discussed. Most of the variables are coded as dummy
variables because these variables are measured on
either a nominal or ordinal level. Some ordinal data
are measured on an interval level. The two pilot
studies, the results of which were used to obtain variables for this research, were also discussed.

The findings of the research will be discussed in
Chapter IV. All the statistical procedures necessary
to empirically test the eight research questions posed
in Chapter II will be discussed. The path coefficients
will be presented and the discriminant functions will
be plotted.

Chapter IV

FINDINGS

In this chapter the findings of the research will
be reported and discussed. Whenever possible, all
three samples will be discussed together for comparative purposes. As mentioned previously, sample 1 consists of 983 cases in which probation officers make a
recommendation.[1] Sample 2 consists of 836 cases in
which the defendants are sentenced without a probation
report.[2] Sample 3 consists of 100 cases from pro-forma
reports, short reports in which the probation officer
neither verifies any information nor makes a recommendation. Nearly all of the defendants in sample 3 are in
remand.

---

[1]Unfortunately, the computer lost four cases from
sample 1, and thus, the total N for this sample is 979
for most analyses.

[2]The majority of defendants at Brooklyn Criminal
Court are sentenced without a probation report. Some
estimate that 80% to 85% are sentenced without a probation report.

In Table 5, the characteristics of the defendants for all three samples are shown.

Table 5

Characteristics of the Defendants

Variable[a]	Sample 1		Sample 2		Sample 3	
	No.[b]	Per.[b]	No.[b]	Per.[b]	No.[b]	Per.[b]
EOD						
White	200	20.4	184	22	4	4
Black	515	52.6	417	49	65	65
Puerto Rican	263	26.9	180	21.5	31	31
Not Known			55	6.6		
AGE						
Under 19	230	23.5	101	12.1	25	25
19 and over	748	76.4	715	85.5	75	75
SEX						
Male	875	89.4	710	84.9	95	95
Female	104	10.6	120	14.4	5	5
MS						
Married	276	28.2	91	10.9		
Not married	694	70.9	168	10.1		
Unknown			576	68.9		

[a]See chapters II and III for an explanation of the symbols.

[b]The number of cases is less than the sample size and less than 100% in certain categories due to missing observations.

Table 5 continued next page

Table 5 (cnt'd)

Characteristics of the Defendants

Variable[a]	Sample 1		Sample 2		Sample 3	
	No.[b]	Per.[b]	No.[b]	Per.[b]	No.[b]	Per.[b]
ES						
Employed schl.	475	48.5	250	29.9		
Unemployed	502	51.3	205	24.5		
Unknown			381	45.6		
PR						
Promises	181	18.5	4	.5	61	61
No Promises	548	55.9	832	99.5	39	39
Unknown	250	25.4				
WA						
Warrants	321	32.8	204	24.4	24	24
No Warrants	432	44.0	632	75.6	76	76
Unknown	226	23.0				
APP						
Poor	145	14.8				
Good	200	20.4				
No Program	634	64.8				
SOC						
category 1	231	23.6	98	11.7	42	42
category 2	713	72.8	363	43.4	57	.57
category 3	33	3.4	373	44.6	1	1

[a]See chapters II and III for an explanation of the symbols.

[b]The number of cases is less than the sample size and less than 100% in certain categories due to missing observations.

Table 5 continued next page

Table 5 (cnt'd)

Characteristics of the Defendants

Variable[a]	Sample 1		Sample 2		Sample 3	
	No.[b]	Per.[b]	No.[b]	Per.[b]	No.[b]	Per.[b]
SFC						
category 1	139	14.2	30	3.6	11	11
category 2	803	81.8	239	28.6	88	88
category 3	35	3.6	565	67.6	1	1
EOC						
White	544	55.6	239	28.6	45	45
Black	149	15.2	81	9.7	29	29
Puerto Rican	68	6.9	38	4.5	16	16
Unknown	196	20.0	464	55.5	7	7
PTS						
Remand	270	27.6	66	7.9		
Out	698	71.3	700	83.7		
Not known			70	8.4		
LS						
Legal Aid	776	79.3	654	78.2		
Legal Aid and Private	1	.1	55	6.6		
Private	161	16.4	87	10.4		
Unknown			40	4.8		
OV						
White v. White	150	15.3	78	9.3	4	4
White v. Black Puerto Rican	11	1.1	6	.7	0	0

[a]See chapters II and III for an explanation of the symbols.

[b]The number of cases is less than the sample size and less than 100% in certain categories due to missing observations.

Table 5 continued next page

Table 5 (cnt'd)

Characteristics of the Defendants

Variable[a]	Sample 1 No.[b] Per.[b]		Sample 2 No.[b] Per.[b]			Sample 3 No.[b] Per.[b]	
Black, P.R. vs. White	391	39.9	158	18.9	41	41	
Black, P.R. vs. Black,P.R.	211	21.6	111	13.3	46	46	
No Victim	196	20.0	464	55.5	9	9	

[a]See Chapters II and III for an explanation of the symbols.

[b]The number of cases is less than the sample size and less than 100% in certain categories due to missing observations.

Characteristics of the Defendants

In Table 5, the characteristics of the defendants for all three samples are shown. All three classes of variables, namely, legal, personal attributes, and relations are shown. The defendants can be described as mainly Black and Puerto Rican, male, and over 19. Concerning those on whom there is information, the majority are unmarried, and in sample 1 slightly more are unemployed or out of school, rather than in school or employed, and in sample 2, slightly more are employed or in school, rather than unemployed or out of school.

Concerning some of the legal variables for which there is information, the majority have no promises attached to their cases in samples 1 and 2, but in sample 3, the majority do have promises. In all three samples for those on whom there is information, the majority don't have any known warrants. In samples 1 and 2, the majority of defendants are out of remand; however, in sample 3, although pre-trial status is not a variable, practically every defendant is in remand. On those for whom there is information, the majority use legal aid, perhaps implying that our

defendants are mainly from lower SES classes, since
there is a financial criterion for legal aid. In
sample 1, for those who were in a prior correctional
program, the majority made a good adjustment rather
than a poor one.

The type of charge for which the defendants are
arrested and convicted is also shown in Table 5. In
samples 1 and 3, both the original and final charges
are mostly in category 2, which consists mainly of
crimes against property. In sample 2, the original
charge is about half in category 2 and half in category 3, but the final charge is mostly in category 3,
which are mostly victimless crimes. A comparison
among the victim and offender-victim categories is
also shown in Table 5. In samples 1 and 3 the majority of victims are White or government agency, e.g.,
welfare or a school, but in sample 2, most of the
charges are victimless. In sample 1, the most frequent offender-victim category is Black, Puerto Rican
vs. White, or government agency. In sample 3, the
most frequent offender-victim category is Black,
Puerto Rican vs. Black, Puerto Rican. In sample 2,
most of the charges are victimless; thus, the most
frequent offender-victim category is No Victim. In
all three samples, the least frequent category is
White versus Black, Puerto Rican. A review of the
literature reveals that crime is mostly an intra-
racial affair.

Prior Record

The mean number of arrests and convictions, the
range of the number of arrests and convictions, the
mean of the seriousness of prior arrests, and the mean
for the disposition of prior convictions are shown for
all three samples in Table 6. There is no information
on convictions for sample 3. The seriousness of prior
arrests was measured on a scale from 1, the most serious to 4, the least serious.[1] Looking at Table 6,
sample 3 has the highest mean number of arrests, and

---

[1]See Chapter III under Scaling of the Variables
for an explanation of this.

84

Table 6

Prior Record

	Sample 1	Sample 2	Sample 3
Arrests-Range	32	40	21
Arrests-Mean No.	3.058	2.517	6.380
Convictions-Range	20	30	
Convictions-Mean No.	1.420	.831	
Seriousness of prior arrests-Mean	2.401	2.922	1.888
Disposition of prior convictions-Mean	2.760	3.361	

sample 2, the lowest mean number of arrests, with sample 1 in-between. The mean number of convictions is greater in sample 1 compared to sample 2. Looking at the mean for the seriousness of prior arrests, sample 3 has the most serious prior arrests and sample 2 the least serious, with sample 1 in-between. Sample 2 has the less severe prior dispositions compared to sample 1. Summarizing, it seems that sample 3 has the worst prior record and sample 2 the least severe prior record, with sample 1 in-between.

Type of Charge

The most frequent type of charge for all three samples is shown in Table 7. This is based on the final charge. Looking at Table 7, petit larceny is the most frequent type of charge for samples 1 and 3, but in sample 2, disorderly conduct is the most frequent type of charge. Assault and drugs are the second and third most frequent types of charges in sample 1. In sample 2 unlicensed driver and intoxicated driver are second and third. In sample 3, assault, stolen property, and weapon tie for second place, and criminal tresspassing is third. This reflects the earlier statement made that sample 2 consists mostly of victimless charges, the ones regarded as least serious in the scaling system.

Table 7

Most Frequent Type

of Charge[a]

Charge	Sample 1 No.	Sample 1 Per.	Sample 2 No.	Sample 2 Per.	Sample 3 No.	Sample 3 Per.
Petit larceny	235	23.9	44	5.3	38	38
Assault	129	13.0	23	2.8	10	10
Drugs	108	10.9	52	6.2	2	2
Stolen property	103	10.5	22	2.6	10	10
Criminal tresspass	89	8.9	33	3.9	9	9
Weapon	84	8.4	21	2.5	10	10
Intoxicated driver	20	2.0	80	9.6	1	1
Unlicensed operator	2	.2	119	14.2		
Harassment	4	.4	57	6.8		
Disorderly conduct	1	.1	262	31.3		

[a]In sample 1, the total number of charges exceeds the number of cases because some defendants have multiple charges.

Recommendations of Probation Officers and

Dispositions of Judges

The recommendations of the probation officers which are followed by the judges are shown in Table 8. This table is controlled for case, since probation officers and judges are sentencing in identical cases. Looking at Table 8, it can be seen that probation officers recommend and judges impose probation first, conditional discharge second, jail third, fine fourth, and unconditional discharge last.

Table 8

Recommendation of Probation Officer by Disposition of Judge

Recommendation of Prob. Off.	Jail	Prob.	Con. disch.	Fine	Uncon. disch.	Total
Jail[b]	188	9	24	1	0	222
	84.7[a]	4.1	10.8	0.5	0.0	22.7
	74.0[a]	2.5	7.9	2.3	0.0	
Probation[c]	35	322	15	5	3	380
	9.2	84.7	3.9	1.3	0.8	38.8
	13.8	91.0	4.9	11.6	13.0	
Cond. disch.	30	21	250	18	5	324
	9.3	6.5	77.2	5.6	1.5	33.1
	11.8	5.9	82.0	41.9	21.7	
Fine	1	2	7	18	0	28
	3.6	7.1	25.0	64.3	0.0	2.9
	0.4	.6	2.3	41.9	0.0	
Uncond. disch.	0	0	9	1	15	25
	0.0	0.0	36.0	4.0	60.0	2.6
	0.0	0.0	3.0	2.3	65.2	
Total	254	354	305	43	23	979
	25.9	36.2	31.2	4.4	2.3	

[a]The top percent is the row, and the bottom percent is the column.

[b]Includes commitment to drug facility as inpatient and time served.

[c]Includes split sentence of 60 days jail and 34 months probation.

The final results indicate that judges impose jail on 254 cases against the 222 jail recommendations of the probation officers, probation 354 times against the 360 recommendations for probation, 305 conditional discharges against the 324 recommendations of the probation officers, fines 43 times against the 28 recommendations of the probation officers, and 23 unconditional discharges against the 25 recommendations of the probation officers. Taking the total number of cases, the judges follow the recommendations of the probation officers 793 times out of 979 times, or about 81% of the time.

Looking at specific sentences in cases of disagreement between judge and probation officer, some dispositions tend toward higher and some toward lower severity sanctions. Totaling the figures, the judges are more punitive in 106 cases and less punitive in 80 cases. In other words, the judges are more punitive 57% of the time and less punitive 43% of the time. This difference is significant at the 95% confidence level.

It seems that after analyzing the date from Table 8, there is remarkable agreement between the recommendations of the probation officers and disposition of the judges both in the percentage of cases followed and in the severity of sanctions imposed.

The dispositions of the judges for all three samples are shown in Table 9. Probation is excluded from sample 2.

Table 9

Dispositions of Judges--Samples 1, 2, 3

Disposition	Sample 1 No.	Per.	Sample 2 No.	Per.	Sample 3 No.	Per.
Jail[a]	254	25.9	173	20.7	79	79
Probation[b]	354	36.2			15	15
Cond. disch.	305	31.2	272	32.5	5	5
Fine	43	4.4	375	44.9	1	1
Uncon. disch.	23	2.3	16	1.9		
Total	979	100.0	836	100.0		

[a]Includes commitment to drug facility as inpatient and time served.

[b]Includes split sentence of 60 days jail and rest of time on probation.

The most frequent disposition is probation for sample 1,
fine for sample 2, and jail for sample 3. The second
most frequent disposition is conditional dishcarge in
samples 1 and 2, and probation in sample 3. The third
most frequent disposition is jail in samples 1 and 2,
and conditional discharge in sample 3. The fourth most
frequent disposition is a fine in samples 1 and 3, and
unconditional discharge in sample 2. An unconditional
discharge is the least most frequent disposition in
sample 1, and although there are no unconditional discharges in sample 3, this is the least frequent disposition for all three samples. Summarizing, it seems
that the most severe sanctions are imposed in sample 3,
and the most leneient sanctions in sample 2, with sample
1 in-between.

Sentence Length

Both the lenth of jail sentences imposed and the
variability of these sentences for Class A and Class B
misdemeanors for all three samples are shown in Table
10.[1] Looking at Table 10 for Class A misdemeanors,
sample 3 has the longest sentences, sample 2 the shortest, with sample 1 in-between. For Class B misdemeanors, sample 1 receives the longest sentence, sample

Table 10

Sentence Length (in months)

Type	Sample 1 Mean	S.D.[a]	Sample 2 Mean	S.D.	Sample 3 Mean	S.D.
Class A[b]	5.1	3	1.9	1.3	7.4	3.02
Class B	2.4	.77	2.2	.9	1.8	.80

[a]S.D. equals the standard deviation

[b]The differences for Class A misdemeanors are
significant as measured by a Z test.

---

[1]Class A misdemeanors legally have a maximum penalty
of one year jail and Class B misdemeanors carry a maximum penalty of three months jail.

89

3 the shortest sentence, with sample 2 in-between.
Looking at the standard deviation for Class A misdemeanors, the variabllity is about the same for samples
1 and 3, but smaller for sample 2. Looking at Class B
misdemeanors, the variability is about the same for
all samples. This analysis indicates the jail sentences are more apt to vary among the defendants in samples
1 and 3 for Class A misdemeanors compared to sample 2,
and that jail sentences are less apt to vary among the
defendants in all three samples for Class B misdemeanors.
While not shown in this table, 14 cases in sample 1
and 14 cases in sample 3 were given one year jail sentences while no one was given a full year jail sentence
in sample 2. Generally, for Class A misdemeanors,
sample 3 receives the most severe sanctions and sample
2 the least severe, with sample 1 in-between.

Fines

The mean amount of fines and the standard deviations associated with these fines are shown in Table
11. Sample 3 is omitted because it had only one case

Table 11

Fines[a,b]

Statistic	Sample 1	Sample 2[c]
Mean	$134.	$50.
Standard dev.	$ 83.	$29.

[a,b]There are statutory limits to the amount of
fines imposed by judges. These fines include both fines
as a separate disposition and fines as a condition of
conditional discharge.

[c]These figures are based on a random sample of 67
cases.

for this disposition. The mean fine for sample 1 is
$134. compared to $50. for sample 2. The standard deviation is greater in sample 1 compared to sample 2,
indicating more variability in sample 1 compared to
sample 2.

Although the sentence length and amount of fines have not been controlled for other variables, they do indicate the differences in severity of sanctions among the three samples.

Correlations

In order to commence research of the type presented here, it is necessary to inspect the zero order correlations in order to determine which variables are highly correlated with the independent variables.[1] This is known as multicollinearity, high correlations between independent variables. Multicollinearity reduces the precision of the estimates in path analysis, so that it is difficult to disentangle the influence of the various independent variables. This loss of precision is due to the fact that there are very large errors associated with these estimates, and these esimtates may be highly correlated with each other. As a result, variables thought not to be signifcant are dropped incorrectly, because these variables might be significant but the sample data have not enabled the researcher to pick up this significance. Dramatic shifts can occur in these estimates with the addition of a few observations. It is possible for two variables not to be highly correlated with each other when they are part of a larger set of variables, yet can form a perfectly collinear set.[2] In this latter case, the determinant of the correlation matrix of independent variables will be close to zero.

Interaction terms can cause high multicollinearity and there are many interactions terms in this research. This researcher wanted to be safe and decided on a cut-off of $\pm$ .70 or above for deleting multicollinear variables. For a pair of highly correlated variables, only one variable was eliminated unless both variables were highly correlated with other variables. In choosing the variable in any one pair to be eliminated, this researcher retained the one which the theoretical perspective of this research indicated as the more important variables. The same set of multicollinear variables were eliminated from both path analysis and

---

[1]See Appendices A, B, and C for a complete list of zero order correlations.

[2]J. Johnson, Econometric Methods, second edition, New York: McGraw Hill, 1972, 160, 163.

discriminant analysis.

In sample 1, the variables X13, White complainant, X14 Black complainant, X16, offender-victim category of White defendant vs. White complainant, X22, the interaction of recommendation of probation officer, number of arrests, seriousness of final charge, X23, the interaction of number of convictions and seriousness of final charge, X25, interaction of employment and marital status, X27, interaction of White complainant and offender-victim category of Black, Puerto Rican defendant vs. White complainant, X32, X33, the interaction of race and number of arrests, and NC, number of convictions, were all eliminated because of multicollinearity. A total of 10 variables were eliminated from a total of 40 independent variables in sample 1.

In sample 2, only four variables were eliminated due to multicollinearity. These were NC, number of convictions, X11 and X12, White and Black complainant respectively. and Y23, the interaction of seriousness of final charge and number of arrests. There are a total of 31 independent variables in sample 2.

In sample 3 the variables Z7, White complainant and Z12, the offender-victim catagory of Black, Puerto Rican defendant versus Black, Puerto Rican complainant were eliminated due to multicollinearity. In addition, the variables Z1, White defendant, and Z10, the offender-victim category of White defendant vs. White complainant were eliminated due to the small number of cases in these two categories. Thus, in sample 3, a total of 4 variables were eliminated from 16 independent variables.

Some of the variables may have unequal variances for each observation of the error, terms, a condition known as heteroskedasticity. However, in this case, the path coefficients are unbiased, but the standard errors of the path coeffieicents may be erroneous.[1] Therefore, the results are not affected.

---

[1] Eric A. Hanushek and John E. Jackson, _Statistical Methods for Social Scientists_, New York: Academic Press 1977, 141-3.

Quantitative Analysis

In this section, the results of both path analysis and discriminant analysis will be presented. Path analysis was performed in three stages, which will be described. Tables showing the direct, indirect and total effects will be presented for significant paths. Discriminant functions will be plotted for samples 1, 2 and 3.

Path Analysis

Path analysis was performed in three stages. In stage one, pre-trial status, recommendation of the probation officer, and disposition of the judge were the dependent variables. All the variables, including the multicollinear variables, but excluding the variables based on theoretical perspectives, were used in stage one of the analysis.[1] When the correlation matrix was printed by SPSS, the multicollinear variables were located and eliminated from further analysis. Then all the paths included in the full models were analyzed in stage one.[2]

Stage two consisted of eliminating all the direct paths which didn't meet two criteria. If a path was not significant on at least a .05 level, and didn't have a magnitude of $\pm$.10 or above, it was eliminated. Both criteria had to be met for a path to be retained in stage two. Stage three involved analyzing the individual paths of probation officers and judges with the highest number of cases in samples 1 & 2, and comparing the results of the individual paths to the path coefficients of the sample as a whole. Sample 3 was not analyzed in stage three because the N for each judge was small, not exceeding 13 for any one judge. The three stages will now be discussed.

---

[1]The reason for including the multicollinear variables at this stage was because SPSS doesn't print correlations for dummy variables without regression analysis. Consequently, there were no grounds for excluding multicollinear variables earlier.

[2]See Tables 2, 3 and 4 for paths included in the full models.

Stage One

There were three dependent variables in stage one for sample 1, namely, pre-trial status, recommendation of probation officer, and disposition of judge. There were three dependent variables in sample 2, namely, remand, out of remand and disposition of judge. There was only one dependent variable in sample 3, namely, disposition of the judge. All the paths included in the full models were analyzed in stage one.[1] However, only those paths which met our two criteria, namely, significance on at least the .05 level and obtained magnitudes of at least $\pm$.10 were retained for stage two of the analysis. The standardized, unstandardized values and the significance level of those direct path coefficients which met the two criteria for retention in stage two of the analysis are shown in Tables 12, 13 and 14.

Looking at Table 12, for sample 1, with X20 pre-trial status, as dependent variable, the paths to NA, number of arrests, X9, X10, warrants, X11, poor adjustment in a prior correctional program and X31, legal aid, met our criteria for inclusion in stage two of the analysis.

With RPO, recommendation of probation officer as dependent variable, the paths to NA, number of arrests, SPA, seriousness of prior arrests, X3, age under 19, or youthful offender, X6, employed or in school, X11, poor adjustment in a prior correctional program, X20, pre-trial status, and the two interaction terms, X28, X29, poor and good adjustment respectively, in a prior correctional program, number of arrests, and seriousness of final charge, met our criteria for inclusion in stage two of the analysis.

With DJ, disposition of judge, as dependent variable, the paths to NA, number of arrests, RPO, recommendation of probation officer, and X20, pre-trial status, met our criteria for inclusion in stage two of the analysis.

A significance test for the equality of regression coefficients was performed for every set of dummy

---

[1]See Tables 2, 3 and 4 for a complete list of paths analyzed in stage one.

Table 12

Standardized, Unstandardized Path Coefficients--

Direct Effects--Sample 1-Stage One

| | Dependent Variable | | | | | |
Indep.Var.	X20 Stan.	Unstan.	RPO Stan.	Unstan.	DJ Stan.	Unstan.
NA	.30**[a]	.34[b]	-.29*	-.66	-.12**	-.29
SPA			.10**	.91		
RPO					.62**	.66
X3			-.15**	-.33		
X6			.11*	.20		
X9	.28**	.27				
X10	.23*	.20				
X11	.18**	.22	-.18**	-.49		
X20			-.22**	-.45	-.17**	-.36
X21	.13**	.14				
X28			.12**	.20		
X29			.11**	.25		

[a]One asterisk indicates significance at the .05 level and two asterisks indicate significance at the .01 level.

[b]All path coefficients are rounded to two places.

variables in the analysis. This is performed to determine if the dummy variables in any set are significantly different from each other. Two models are analyzed, a full model and a reduced model. A full model is represented by a B, or regression slope for every dummy variable in a set. Thus, the full model is:

$$Y = B_o + B_1 X_1 + B_2 X_2 + B_3 X_3 + E$$

where Y is the predicted value, B_o is the intercept, and B_1, B_2, B_3 are the regression slopes, X_1, X_2, X_3 the independent variables, and E is the error term.

In the reduced model, a new variable is created by the addition of all the independent variables and the Beta is factored. The reduced model is represented as

$$Y = B_o + B (X_1 + X_2 + X_3),$$

where Y is the predicted variable, B_o is the intercept,
B is the slope for the new variable and X_1, X_2, and X_3
are the independent variables. The error term is dropped.

An F test is performed to determine the significance between the R^2 of the full model and the R^2 of the
reduced model. In this research, every set of dummy
variables in all three stages of path analysis for all
three samples was analyzed by the test for the equality
of the regression coefficient. For example in the full
model, the dependent variables were regressed against
the dummy variables, X13, X14, X15, ethnicity of the
complainant, with a regression slope for each of the
three independent variables, and in the reduced model,
the dependent variables were regressed against a new
variable formed by the addition of X13, X14, X15, with
one regression slope, and the differences between the
full and reduced models were analyzed by means of an F
test. All the results for all sets of dummy variables
for all three samples in all three stages showed no
significant differences in the R^2s of the reduced and
full models. All the regression coefficients in every
set of dummy variables are not signifcantly different
from each other.[1] This test will be discussed further
in stage three of path analysis.

The results of the analysis for sample 2 are shown
in Table 13.

There are three dependent variables in sample 2.
With Y21, remand, as dependent variable, the paths to
SFC, seriousness of final charge, Y16, the offender-
victim category of Black, Puerto Rican vs. White complainant, and Y17, the offender-victim category of
Black, Puerto Rican vs. Black, Puerto Rican, met our
criteria for inclusion in stage two of the analysis.
With Y22, out of remand, as dependent variable, the
paths to SOC, seriousness of original charge, SFC,
seriousness of final charge, NA, number of arrests, DPC,
disposition of prior convictions, Y14, the offender-
victim category of White defendant vs. White complainant, Y16, the offender-victim category of Black,
Puerto Rican defendant vs. White complainant, and X17,

[1]Samprit Chatterjie and Bertram Price, Regression
by Example, New York: John Wiley and Company, 1977,
66-8.

the offender-victim category of Black, Puerto Rican defendant vs. Black, Puerto Rican complainant met our criteria for inclusion in stage two of the analysis.

Table 13

Standardized, Unstandardized Path Coefficients

Direct Effects--Sample 2

Stage One

| | Dependent Variable | | | | | |
Indep.Var.	Y21 Stan.	Unstan.	Y22 Stan.	Unstan.	DJ Stan.	Unstan.
SOC	a	b	-.11*	-.60		
SFC	-.19**	-.89	.20**	.13	.12**	.25
NA			-.25**	-.22		
DPC			.11*	.35		
Y14			-.10*	-.13		
Y16	.15*	.10	-.12*	-.11		
Y17	.17*	.13	-.13**	-.14		
Y22					.69**	2.17

[a]One asterisk indicates significance at the .05 level, and two asterisks indicate significance at the .01 level.

[b]All path coefficients are rounded to two places.

The results of stage one for sample 3 are shown in Table 14. There is only one dependent variable in sample 3, DJ, or disposition of judge. It can be seen from Table 14 that NA, number of arrests, was the only path which met the criteria for inclusion in stage two of the analysis.

Table 14

Standardized, Unstandardized Path Coefficients

Direct Effects--Sample 3--Stage One

Independent Variable	Dependent Variable --DJ	
	Stand.	Unstand.
NA	$-.28*$[a]	$-.40$[b]

[a]One asterisk indicates significance at the .05 level.

[b]All path coefficients are rounded to two places.

Summarizing the results of stage one it can be seen that failure of many paths to meet our two criteria resulted in elimination of many paths for stage two of the analysis. This is the reduced model for stage two. In stage two, there are 12 independent variables for sample 1, 9 independent variables for sample 2, and only 1 independent variable for sample 3.

Stage Two

As mentioned previously, only paths which met our
two criteria, namely, significance on at least a .05
level and magnitudes of at least $\pm$.10 were retained for
stage two. There were a few exceptions, which will be
mentioned in analyzing the results. However, even if a
path didn't meet the criteria for inclusion in stage
two, if the zero order correlation between the two variables was significant on at least a .05 level and had a
magnitude of at least $\pm$.10, the indirect effect of the
eliminated path was retained. The results of stage
two for sample 1 are shown in Table 15.

Looking at Table 15, for X20, pre-trial status as
dependent variable, one can see that NA, number of arrests, has the greatest direct effect, with a value of
.27, explaining about 6% of the variance. The indirect
effect is .10, and the total effect is .37, explaining
about 14% of the variance. Since the sign is positive,
this means the more the arrests, the more the defendant
is in remand.

The next greatest direct effect on pre-trial status is X11, poor adjustment in a prior correctional program, with a value of .20, explaining 4% of the variance.
The indirect effect is .10 and the total effect is .30,
explaining about 9% of the variance. Since the sign is
positive, this indicates that the more the defendant
has a poor adjustment in a prior correctional program,
the more he is in remand.

The next greatest direct effect on pre-trial status is X21, legal aid, with a value of .13, explaining
about 1-1/2% of the variance. The indirect effect is
.08 and the total effect is .21, explaining about 4% of
the variance. Since the sign is positive, this indicates that the more legal aid is employed, the more
one is in remand.

The next greatest direct effect on pre-trial status is X9, warrants, with a value of .12, explaining
about 1% of the variance. The indirect effect is .13
and the total effect is .25, explaining about 6% of the
variance. Since the sign is positive, this indicates
that the more the defendant has had one or more warrants, the more he is in remand.

Two variables, X6, employment, and X10, no warrants, each has direct effects which explains less than
1% of the variance. The indirect effect of X6 on X20

99

Table 15

Path Analysis--Direct, Indirect, Total

Effects--R^2←-Sample 1

Stage Two

| | Dependent Variable | | | | | | | | |
Indep. Var.	X20 Dir.	Indir.	Tot.	RPO Dir.	Indir.	Tot.	DJ Dir.	Indir.	Tot.
NA	(.31)ᵃ .27**ᵇ	.10	.37	(-.88) -.30**	-.05	-.35	(-.21) -.09**	-.28	-.37
SPA		-.26	-.26	(.10) .11**	.18	.29		.28	.28
RPO							(.66) .64**	.02	.66
X3				(-.33) -.15**	-.08	-.07		-.04	-.04
X4		.06	.06		-.08	-.08			
X6	(-.60) -.07*	-.08	-.15	(.24) .13**	.07	.20		.20	.20
X9	(.11) .12	.13	.25		-.19	-.19		-.18	-.18
X10	(.17) .02	-.13	-.11		.12	.12		.12	.12
X11	(.25) .20**	.10	.30	(-.50) -.19**	-.11	-.30		-.28	-.28
X18		.03	.03		-.06	-.06		-.08	-.08
X20				(-.49) -.24**	-.18	-.42	(-.36) -.17**	-.30	-.47
X21	(.15 .13**	.08	.21		-.16	-.16		-.19	-.19
X24					-.24	-.24		-.26	-.26

ᵃThe values inside the parentheses are the unstandardized path coefficients and the values outside the parentheses are the standardized path coefficients.

ᵇOne asterisk indicates significance at the .05 level and two asterisks indicate significance at the .01 level.

ᶜAll path coefficients are rounded to two places.

Table 15 (cnt'd)

Indep. Var.	Dir.	X20 Indir.	Tot.	Dir.	RPO Indir.	Tot.	Dir.	DJ Indir.	Tot.
				$(.22)^a$					
X28	.26	.26		.14**	-.36	-.22		-.28	-.28
				(.24)					
X29				.11**	-.09	.02		-.00	-.00
X30					.08	.08		.18	.18
R^2	$.23**^c$			$.30*^b$			.58**		

[a]The values inside the parentheses are the un-standardized path coefficients and the values outside the parentheses are the standardized path coefficients.

[b]One asterisk indicates significance at the .05 level and two asterisks indicate significance at the .01 level.

[c]All path coefficients are rounded to two places.

is -.08, and the total effect is -.15, explaining about 2% of the variance. Since the sign is negative, this indicates that the more one is in remand, the less he is employed or in school. The indirect effect of X10, no warrants, on X20, remand, is -.13 and the total effect is -.11, explaining about 1% of the variance. Since the sign is negative, this means that the more there are no warrants, the less the defendant is in remand. Although X6, employment, didn't meet our criteria for inclusion in stage two, it was included in stage two because this researcher believed that it might contribute to an explanation of pre-trial status (see Table 12).

There are indirect effects on X20. The variables X4, male and X18, the offender-victim category of Black, Puerto Rican defendant versus White complainant, explained seprately less than 1% of the variance. The variable SPA, seriousness of prior arrests and X28, poor adjustment in a prior correctional program, number of arrests, and seriousness of final charge, each has an indirect effect of .26, explaining about 6-1/2% of the variance. Since the sign is negative for SPA, this

101

indicates that more serious prior arrests are associated with remand. Since the sign for X28 is positive, this indicates that number arrests and seriousness of final charge interact with poor adjustment to produce remand.

The R^2 for pre-trial status is low, .23. This analysis emphasizes the importance of legal variables for pre-trial status, namely, the number of arrests, poor adjustment in a prior correctional program, and warrants. The more the arrests, the more a poor adjustment in a prior correctional program, the more the warrants, the more a defendant will be in remand. Use of legal aid is also associated with remand. Perhaps legal aid lawyers are obliged to promise the judge that most criminal defendants will be remanded, or perhaps legal aid lawyers don't defend as vigorously as private lawyers.

Looking at RPO, recommendations of probation officers as dependent variable, it is seen that NA, number of arrests, has the greatest direct effect on RPO with a value of -.30, explaining 9% of the variance. The total effect is -.35 , explaining about 12% of the variance. Since the sign is negative, this indicates that the more the arrests, the more severe the recommendations of the probation officer. The second greatest direct effect on RPO is X20, pre-trial status, with a value of -.24 explaining about 5-1/2% of the variance. The total effect of X20 is -.42, explaining about 17% of the variance. Since the sign is negative, this indicates that the more one is in remand, the more severe the recommendation. The third greatest direct effect is X11, poor adjustment in a prior correctional program, with a value of -.19, explaining about 3-1/2% of the variance, and a total effect of -.30, explaining about 9% of the variance. Since the sign is negative, this means that more severe recommendations are associated with poor adjustment in a prior correctional program.

The three next greatest direct effects on recommendations of probation officers are X3, age under 19, X28, interaction of poor adjustment in a prior correctional program, number of arrests and seriousness of final charge, and X6, employment. The direct effect explains about 2% of the variance for each variable, and the total effects explain from less than 1% of the variance for X3, age under 19, to 5% of the variance for X28, the interaction variable. Age seems to have a

102

small impact on recommendations of probation officers. It seems that the number of arrests and seriousness of final charge interact with poor adjustment in a prior correctional program to produce a more severe recommendation, because the sign of the total effect is negative (see Chapter III for the coding of the variables). The sign of X6, employment, is positive, which indicates that lenient recommendations are associated with employment, or being in school.

The next two greatest direct effects are SPA, seriousness of prior arrests, and X29, interaction of good adjustment in a prior correctional program, number of arrests, and seriousness of final charge. The direct effect of each explains about 1% of the variance, but the total effect of SPA explains about 8% of the variance, and the total effect of X29 explains less than 1% of the variance. The sign of SPA is positive, indicating that more lenient recommendations are associated with less serious prior arrests, and more severe dispositions with more serious prior arrests. The total effect of X29, the interaction variable, is minimal, but the direct effect is positive, which means that a good adjustment in a prior correctional program interacts with number of arrests and seriousness of final charge to produce a more lenient decision.

There are other variables which have only indirect effects. These are X24, interaction of remand and promises, X21, legal aid, X30, interaction of White defendant and employment, X9, X10, warrants, and X18, the offender-victim category of Black, Puerto Rican defendant versus White complainant. The indirect effects each explains from less than 1% of the variance to about 6% of the variance. The sign of X24 is negative, indicating that promises interact with remand to produce more severe recommendations; the sign of X21, legal aid, is negative, indicating that legal aid is associated with more severe recommendations; the signs of X9, X10, warrants, indicate that warrants are associated with more severe recommendations. None of the ethnic categories, X18, X30, explains as much as 1% of the variance.

The variables in sample 1 for RPO, recommendations of the probation officer, were entered in stepwise fashion. All the legal variables were entered first. This included all variables except X3, age and X6, employment. The R^2 for the legal variables was .27. With the inclusion of X3, age and X6, employment, the extra-legal variables, the R^2 was .30. This indicates

103

that legal variables explain a much greater proportion of variance, and the addition of extra-legal variables only adds about 3% to the total R^2. However, this difference is significant at the .05 level as measured by an F test.

Summarizing the results for RPO, recommendation of probation officer, one can say that the three most important factors for recommendation of probation officer are number of arrests, pre-trial status and poor adjustment in prior correctional program. These are legal variables. The more arrests a defendant has, the more he is in remand, and the more he has made a poor adjustment in a prior correctional program, the more severe the recommendation of a probation officer. Moreover, the number of arrests and seriousness of final charge interact with poor adjustment to produce a severe recommendation. The number of arrests and seriousness of final charge, however, interact with a good adjustment to produce a more lenient recommendation. It seems that if a defendant is in remand, he will be recommended for a severe sentence. Perhaps there is something about being in remand that affects probation officers' decisions. It also seems that probation officers look at the seriousness of prior arrests, and the more serious the prior arrests, the more severe the recommendation, and the less serious the prior arrests, the more lenient the recommendation. If a defendant has a history of serious crimes, this will work negatively for him when probation officers make a recommendation.

The total R^2 is .30. There is a lot of unexplained variation. However, based on what is explained, it seems that legal variables affect recommendations of probation officers more than extra-legal variables, such as age and employment. Based on the analysis, it seems that many factors have a small impact on recommendations because no direct effect explained more than 9% of the variance, and no total effect explained more than 18% of the variance.

Looking at Table 15, DJ, disposition of the judge, one sees that RPO, recommendation of the probation officer, has the greatest impact on disposition of judge, with a value of .64, explaining about 41% of the variance. The indirect effect is .02, and the total effect is .66, explaining about 44% of the variance. Since the sign is positive, this indicates that severe dispositions are associated with severe recommendations and lenient dispositions are associated with lenient recommendations.

The next greatest direct effect on DJ, disposition of judge, is X20, pre-trial status, with a value of -.17, explaining about 3% of the variance. The indirect effect is -.30, and the total effect is -.47, explaining about 22% of the variance. Since the sign is negative, this indicates that the more severe dispositions of the judge are associated with remand.

The variable with the least greatest direct effect on disposition of the judge is NA, number of arrests, with a value of .09, explaining less than 1% of the variance. However, the indirect effect is -.28, and the total effect is -.37, explaining about 14% of the variance. Since the sign is negative, this indicates that the greater the number of arrests, the more severe the disposition of the judge.

Several variables have indirect effects. These variables are SPA. seriousness of prior arrests, X3, age, X6, employment, X9, and X10, warrants, X11, poor adjustment in a prior correctional program, X18, offender-victim category of Black, Puerto Rican defendant versus White complainant, X21, legal aid, X24, interaction of remand and promises, X28, interaction of poor adjustment in a prior correctional program, number of arrests, and seriousness of final charge, and X30, interaction of White defendant and employment. The indirect effects each explains from less than 1% of the variance, X18, X3, to about 8% of the variance, X28, SPA. The signs indicate that more serious prior arrests, warrants, poor adjustment in a prior correctional program, age under 19, and legal aid are associated with severe dispositions and employment or being in school is associated with more lenient dispositions. Promises interact with remand and number of arrests, seriousness of final charge interact with a poor adjustment to produce a more severe disposition. The interaction of White defendant and employment is associated with more lenient dispositions.

Summarizing the results for disposition of judge, it seems that the recommendations of probation officers have the greatest direct effect on disposition of the judges. This is in agreement with the earlier analysis of the percentage of recommendations which are followed by the judges, which indicated remarkable agreement between recommendation and disposition. It seems judges depend on the probation officer to make a sentencing disposition. The proportion of variance explained is

105

at least 40% for this one factor. In addition to recommendation of probation officer, judges will sentence more
severely if the defendant is in remand. Perhaps judges
are affected negatively by pre-trial status, or perhaps
they are obliged to sentence defendants in remand because
of negotiations with the district attorney. Also, although the number of arrests do not affect judges' decisions directly, perhaps because they rely on recommendations, the number of arrests indirectly affects the
decisions.

The total R^2 for disposition of judges is .58,
which is higher than the R's of pre-trial status and
recommendations of probation officers. The higher R^2
is the result of the great impact of recommendations of
probation officers on their sentencing decisions.

It is possible to delete further paths from this
analysis if they fail to meet statistical significance
or fail to have a magnitude of at least $\pm.10$. Looking
at Table 15, for X20, pre-trial status, it is possible
to delete the paths to X6 and X10; for RPO, it is not
possible to delete any path; and for DJ, it is possible
to delete the path to NA, and reanalyze the data with
the remaining paths. However, this was not done here
because it only involved three paths, and it was believed that this type of analysis would not reveal anything substantially different.

The unstandardized path coefficients can also be
analyzed. The unstandardized path coefficients show
how much change in the dependent variable is associated
with change in the independent variable. Looking at
Table 15 for X20, pre-trial status, the unstandardized
path coefficient is .31 for NA, number of arrests. This
indicates that for every unit change in number of arrests, there will be a .31 unit increase in pre-trial
status. Looking at RPO, recommendation of probation
officer, as dependent variable, the unstandardized
path coefficient for NA, number of arrests is -.68.
This means that for every unit change in number of arrests the recommendations of probation officers will
decrease by .68, since the sign is negative. Looking
at disposition of judge, as dependent variable, the
unstandardized path coefficient for recommendation of
probation officer is .66, which means that for every
unit change in recommendation of probation officer,
the disposition of the judge will increase by .66 units.
The other unstandardized path coefficients can be
analyzed in the same way.

Summarizing the results of sample 1, one can say
that legal variables, namely, number of arrests, pre-
trial status, and adjustment in a prior correctional
program, have a great effect on sentencing decisions.
However, the greatest effect in the sentencing process
is the recommendation of the probation officer, since
this has the highest path value. The extra-legal variables, age and employment, have a small effect on sentencing decisions. Warrants and legal aid both affect
pre-trial status directly, and sentencing decisions indirectly, indicating their unimportance for sentencing.
The small indirect effect of the ethnic categories, in
this researcher's opinion, is of no consequence.

The results of stage two for sample 2 are shown in
Table 16. Looking at Y21, remand, as dependent variable, one can see that SFC, serious of final charge,
has the greatest direct effect on remand status, explaining about 3-1/2% of the variance. The indirect effect
is -.04, and the total effect is -.23, explaining about
5% of the variance. Since the sign is negative, this
indicates that the more one is in remand, the more
severe the final charge. The variables, Y16, offender-
victim category of Black, Puerto Rican defendant versus White complainant and Y17, the offender-victim
category of Black, Puerto Rican defendant versus Black,
Puerto Rican complainant have direct effects on remand
of .10 and .11 respectively, each explaining about 1%
of the variance. The total effect of each variable
only explains about 1% of the variance. Since the sign
is positive, this indicates that remand is associated
with those offender-victim categories.

The R^2 is .07, indicating a lot of unexplained
variance. Since the path values of the two offender-
victim categories are very low, each explaining about
1% of the variance, and since it involves two categories, this researcher doubts that this proves any
kind of ethnic discrimination.

Looking at Y22, out of remand, one sees that NA,
the number of arrests, has the greatest effect on out of
remand, with a value of -.26, explaining about 13% of
the variance. Since the sign is negative, this indicates that the more one is out of remand, the less the
number of arrests.

Table 16

Path Analysis--Direct, Indirect, Total Effects--

R^2--Sample 2--Stage Two

Indep. Var.	Y21			Dependent Variable Y22			DJ		
	Dir.	Indir.	Tot.	Dir.	Indir.	Tot.	Dir.	Indir.	Tot.
SOC				(-.63) -.12**[a]	.24	.12		.24	.24
SFC	(-.90)**[b] -.19[c]	-.04	-.23	(.13) .20**	.06	.26	(.40) .19**	.17	.36
NA				(-.23) -.26**	-.10	-.36		-.36	-.36
SPA					-.16	-.16		.24	.24
DPC				(.33) .10*	.21	.31		.31	.31
Y2								.14	.14
Y9								-.16	.16
Y14				(-.96) -.08*	.04	-.04		-.04	-.04
Y16	(.72) .10*	.02	.12	(-.11) (-.11)**	0	-.11		-.16	-.16
Y17	(.91) .11**	.02	.13	(-.13) -.12**	.02	-.10		-.16	-.16
Y18					-.10	-.10		-.19	-.19
Y21							(.39) .09**	-.35	-.44
Y22							(2.3) .73**	-.01	.72
R^2	.07**			.19**			.56**		

[a]All path coefficients are rounded to two places.

[b]The values inside the parentheses are the unstandardized path coefficients and the values outside the parentheses are the standardized path coefficients.

[c]One asterisk indicates significance at the .05 level and two asterisks indicate significance at the .01 level.

The next three greatest direct effects on out of
remand are SFC, seriousness of final charge, SOC, seriousness of original charge, and DPC, disposition of
prior convictions, with path values of .20, -.12, and
.10 respectively. The total effects vary from .31 for
disposition of prior convictions, explaining about 9½%
of the variance, to .26 for seriousness of final
charge, explaining about 1% of the variance. The
signs of the total effects indicate that more lenient
prior convictions and less serious original and final
charges are associated with being out of remand.

Three offender-victim categories, Y14, White
defendant versus White complainant and Y17, Black,
Puerto Rican defendant versus Black, Puerto Rican complainant have direct effects of -.08. -.11, and -.12,
respectively, each one explaining about 1% of the variance. The total effect varies from -.04 to -.11,
each one explaining no more than 1% of the variance.
The signs are negative, indicating that the more one
is out of remand, the less a defendant is in each of
the three offender-victim categories.

Two variables have indirect effects on Y22, out
of remand, namely SPA, seriousness of prior arrests,
and Y18, legal aid. The indirect effect of SPA is
-.16, explaining about 2% of the variance and the
indirect effect of Y18 is -.10, explaining about 1% of
the variance. Both signs are negative, indicating
that being out of remand is associated with more serious prior arrests and less use of legal aid. It is
somewhat surprising that being out of remand is associated with more serious prior arrests, but the effect
is only indirect and the value is low.

Summarizing the results of Y22, out of remand, it
seems that the legal variables, namely, number of arrests, seriousness of original and final charge, and
disposition of prior convictions will determine whether or not a defendant will be out of remand. The offender-victim categories, in this researcher's opinion, show no evidence of discrimination in pre-trial
status, because three offender-victim categories are
invovled, and the path values are quite low. The
total R^2 is .19, indicating a lot of unexplained variation.

Looking at DJ, disposition of judge as dependent
variable, one sees that Y22, out of remand, has the
greatest direct effect on disposition of judge, with

a value of .73, explaining about 53% of the variance.
The total effect is .72. Since the sign is positive,
this indicates that the more one is out of remand, the
more lenient the disposition of the judge. The next
greatest direct effect is SFC, seriousness of final
charge, with a value of .19, explaining about 3½% of
the variance, and a total effect of .36, explaining
about 13% of the variance. The positive sign indicates that more lenient dispositions are associated
with less serious final charges. The third greatest
direct effect is Y21, remand, with a value of .09,
explaining less than 1% of the variance, but with a
total effect of -.44, explaining about 19% of the variance. The negative sign indicates that more lenient
dispositions of judges are associated with not being
in remand.

Several variables have indirect effects. These
variables are NA, number of arrests, SPA, seriousness
of prior arrests, DPC, disposition of prior convictions, Y2, Black defendant, Y9, unemployed, Y14, the
offender-victim category of White versus White, Y16,
the offender-victim category of Black, Puerto Rican
versus White, Y17, the offender-victim category of
Black, Puerto Rican versus Black, Puerto Rican and
Y18, legal aid. The indirect effects each varies from
-.04 to -.36, explaining from less than 1% of the variance to about 13% of the variance. The signs indicate that more lenient dispositions are associated
with fewer arrests, less serious prior arrests, more
lenient prior dispositions, less unemployment, less
use of legal aid, being a Black defendant, and more
severe dispositions with being in one of the three offender-victim categories.

Summarizing for DJ, disposition of the judge, one
can say that pre-trial status has the greatest impact
on the judge's decision. If a defendant is out of
remand, his chances of receiving a lenient disposition
are very good. Since probation is excluded, this
means that a defendant out of remand in sample 2 will
probably receive a conditional discharge or fine for
his crime. Next to pre-trial status, a less serious
charge will mean a lenient sentence. It has already
been stated that most charges in sample 2 (Table 7)
are victimless charges, charges considered the least
serious. In the researcher's opinion, the small indirect effects of Y2, Black defendant, and Y14, Y16, Y17,
the offender-victim categories of White versus White,

110

Black, Puerto Rican versus White, and Black, Puerto Rican versus Black, Puerto Rican are too small to prove ethnic discrimination. The R^2 is .56, due to the influence of Y22.

Just as in sample 1, paths which didn't meet statistical significance at the .05 level or have a magnitude of ±.10 could have been deleted from stage two and the remaining paths could have been reanalyzed. However, just as in sample 1, the researcher decided against this, because only two paths, Y14 for Y21 and Y21 for DJ, were involved, and this researcher didn't believe that anything would change by this type of analysis.

Just as in sample 1, the unstandardized path coefficients can be analyzed to see how much of a unit change in the independent variable is associated with a unit change in the dependent variable. The largest unstandardized path coefficient is Y22, out of remand, for DJ, disposition of judge, with a value of 2.3 indicating that every unit change out of remand is associated with 2.3 unit increases in disposition of the judge. This is a big impact, and shows the large effect Y22 has on DJ. The other unstandardized path coefficients can be analyzed in the same way.

Summarizing the results for sample 2 as a whole, two factors, pre-trial status and seriousness of final charge, are quite important for dispositions. Seriousness of original and final charge are important for pre-trial status in sample 2, but they are unimportant for pre-trial status in sample 1. Number of arrests are important for pre-trial status in both samples 1 and 2. In sample 1, warrants and legal aid are important for pre-trial status, but in sample 2, warrants are unimportant and legal aid only indirectly affects pre-trial status. In sample 1, pre-trial status has a lesser impact on dispositions than in sample 2, and seriousness of final charge is unimportant for sentencing. In both samples 1 and 2, one factor, recommendation of probation officer in sample 1 and pre-trial status in sample 2, has the greatest effect on sentencing outcomes.

111

The results of stage two for sample 3 are presented in Table 17. One can see that NA, number of arrests, is the only variable which has a direct effect. The results indicate that the direct effect is -.29, explaining about 8% of the variance, indicating that more severe dispositions are associated with a greater number of arrests. Seriousness of prior

Table 17

Path Analysis--Direct, Indirect

Total Effects--R^2--Sample 3--Stage Two

| Indep. Var. | Dependent Variable--DJ | | Total |
	Direct	Indirect	
NA	$(-.04)$ $-.29*^a$	0	$-.29^c$
SPA		.07	.07
R^2	$.08**^b$		

[a]The values inside parentheses are the unstandardized values, and the values outside the parentheses are the standardized values.

[b]Two asterisks indicate significance at the .01 level, and one asterisk indicates significance at the .05 level.

[c]All path coefficients are rounded to two decimal places.

arrests has an indirect effect, but explains less than 1% of the variance. The unstandardized path coefficient is -.04, and the r^2 is .08, indicating a lot of unexplained variance. This again reveals the importance of number of arrests for disposition of the judge.

Summarizing the results of stage two, one can see the importance of legal variables and their direct and indirect effects on dispositions. The two greatest impacts on the sentencing process are RPO, recommendation of probation officer in sample 1 and Y22, pre-trail status, in sample 2. However, pre-trail status is also very important in sample 1 because this also affects recommendations and dispositions both directly and indirectly. Defendants in remand receive more severe dispositions, both in samples 1 and 2, and also in sample 3, since most of the defendants in sample 3 are in remand. Seriousness of final charge is very important in sample 2. Seriousness of prior arrest influences probation officers' recommendations directly in sample 1 and indirectly the judge in samples 1, 2 and 3, and disposition of prior convictions has an impact in sample 2. The number of arrests was important all the way through because this affected pre-trail status directly in samples 1 and 2, and recommendation of probation officer directly in sample 1, and the judges both directly and indirectly in samples 1 and 2, and the judge directly in sample 3. In sample 1, a poor adjustment in a prior correctional program, alone, and in interaction with number of arrests and seriousness of final charge, had a strong impact on pre-trail status and recommendation of probation officer and indirectly affected the judge in sample 1.

It seems that samples 1 and 2 are sorted into two groups, one with lenient dispositions and one with more severe dispositions. Probation is excluded from sample 2, and fine is the most frequent disposition in sample 2 (see Table 9). Most of the defendants in sample 2 are charged with victimless crimes, and these are the charges associated with being out of remand, and less serious charges and out of remand are associated with lenient dispositions. In sample 1, however, jail is given more frequently than in sample 2 (see Table 9), and a different set of factors are operating here than in sample 2. For example, recommendation of probation officer is important in sample 1 but not in sample 2. Seriousness of final charge is important in sample 2, but not in sample 1. Pre-trail status is much more important in sample 2 than in sample 1. Employment has a small impact in sample 1, but is not important in sample 2. It seems that a disposition which a defendant receives depends to a certain extent on whether or not he is given a probation report.

Stage Three

In this section, stage three of the path analysis will be presented. A method will be presented which tests for consistency in sentencing. Consistency in

113

Table 18

Standardized, Unstandardized Path Coefficients--R^2--

Probation Officers--RPO Dependent Variable--Sample 1--Stage Three

Prob. Off.	No. of Cases	NA	SPA	X3	X6	X11	X20	X28	X29	R^2
						Independent Variable[b]				
1	56	-.32 (-.57)	.15 (.12)	-.22 (-.39)	.16 (.28)	-.15 (-.32)	-.29 (-.56)	.17 (.34)	.18 (.49)	.35
2	56	-.44** (-.21)	.04 (.38)	-.35** (-.86)	.17 (.35)	-.79* (-2.2)	-.22* (-.52)	.57 (.21)	-.01 (-.39)	.52*
3	62	-.41** (-.87)	-.10 (-.81)	-.03 (-.60)	.25** (.44)	.17 (-.41)	.24 (-.46)	-.05 (-.93)	.08 (.20)	.40*
4	47	-.14 (-.35)	.09 (.72)	.03 (.70)	.17 (.31)	.07 (.14)	.27 (-.49)	-.16 (-.26)	-.08 (-.24)	.3?
5	69	-.48* (-.90)	.12 (.11)	-.08 (.21)	.13 (.22)	.09 (.25)	-.27* (-.57)	.19 (.21)	.22 (.51)	.37*
6	57	-.24 (-.76)	.12 (.12)	-.38** (-.86)	.23 (.45)	.09 (.25)	.20 (-.43)	-.21 (-.11)	.01 (.33)	.41*
7	56	-.27 (-.39)	.21 (.20)	-.20 (-.45)	.18 (.36)	-.27 (-.64)	.06 (-.12)	.23 (.14)	-.01 (-.47)	.30
8	57	-.24 (-.49)	.02 (.18)	-.25* (-.49)	.03 (.55)	-.06 (-.19)	-.50** (-.92)	-.06 (-.31)	.05 (.13)	.37*
9	75	-.44** (-.13)	.11 (.10)	-.11 (-.27)	.25* (.52)	-.28 (-.90)	-.03 (-.59)	.12 (.50)	.13 (.27)	.44*
10	57	-.33 (-.94)	.12 (.92)	-.09 (-.19)	-.14 (-.23)	-.24 (-.53)	-.23 (-.44)	-.01 (-.13)	.08 (.15)	.30*
Sample 1	979	-.30** (-.68)	.11** (.10)	-.15** (-.33)	.13** (.24)	-.19** (-.50)	-.24** (-.49)	.14** (.22)	.11 (.24)	.30**

a One asterisk indicates significance at the .05 level and two asterisks indicate significance at the .01 level. Values inside parentheses are unstandardized and values outside parentheses are standardized. All path values are rounded to two places.

b See Table 1 for a complete list of variables.

sentencing, as mentioned in Chapter II, is defined as the handling of similar cases in similar ways, or equal sentences for equal cases. Consistency can also be operationalized. One way to test consistency is to compare the individual path coefficients of judges and probation officers to the path coefficients of the sample as a whole, and to test the differences among these path coefficients with an F test. If the path coefficients of individual judges and probation officers are similar, one can infer consistency in sentencing.

Consistency was tested in samples 1 and 2 only. In sample 3, the highest N was 13 for two judges, and most of the judges had N's of 4 or 5. It was decided that this was too small a sample size to test for consistency in sample 3.

Ten probation officers and eight judges in sample 1 and six judges in sample 2 with the highest number of cases were analyzed by means of path analysis. The individual path coefficients of the probation officers and judges were compared to the path coefficients of samples 1 and 2 as a whole. The probation officers and judges were not selected on a random basis, but were the ones with the highest number of cases. The same variables in the same order which were used in stage two of path analysis were used to analyze the path coefficients of the probation officers and judges in stage three.

The results for the ten probation officers are shown in Table 18. Based on the signs of the Betas, and the magnitudes, there is remarkable consistency with some variation among the ten probation officers in sample 1. For example, all the signs for NA, number of arrests, and X20, pre-trail status, are negative. The number of arrests is first in importance in sample 1 as a whole, and this is generally true for all ten probation officers with a few exceptions. For example, probation officer number 2 places X11, poor adjustment, first; probation officer number 6 places X3, age, first, and probation officer number 8 places X20, remand, first in importance. The unstandardized path coefficients do vary among the probation officers. For example, for poor adjustment, X11, the unstandardized path coefficient for sample 1 as a whole is -.50, but the unstandardized path coefficients among the ten probation officers vary from a low of .14 to a high of 2.2. Generally, however, there is consistency among the ten probation officers.

115

A test for the equality of regression coefficients was performed on the Betas of the individual probation officers. This was the same kind of test which was performed on the sets of dummy variables in stages one and two of the path analysis. The full model utilized each Beta for each probation officer for each independent variable as a separate variable and the reduced model combined all the values of each independent variable for each probation officer into a separate variable. For example, for NA, number of arrests, the full model utilized each Beta for NA for each probation officer as a separate variable, ten variables total, and the reduced model combined all ten values of NA into one variable, and the results were compared. This same type of analysis was done for all the other variables.

The R^2s of the full model and reduced model were compared by means of an F test. The results revealed that all the regression coefficients were not significantly different from each other. This means that probation officers are consistent; they evaluate similar cases in similar ways.

Just as in sample 1, a step-wise procedure was used to determine the importance of legal and extra-legal variables. This would also partially test if the defendants receive individual attention in the disposition of their cases, because extra-legal variables generally are not supposed to enter into sentencing decisions. This same type of analysis was done for sample 1 as a whole, and it was found that extra-legal variables add only about 3% of the total R^2. The results of the step-wise procedure for the ten probation officers are shown in Table 19.

One can see by looking at Table 19 that very little additional variance is explained by the addition of the two extra-legal variables, age and employment. The highest difference is .15, and the lowest difference is .01. None of the differences is significant as measured by an F test. In sample 1 as a whole, however the difference in the R2 was significant at the .05 level. This analysis proves that legal variables are more important than extra-legal variables among the ten probation officers. In Chapter V, there will be a discussion on whether or not defendants receive individual attention in the disposition of their cases.

The same type of analysis was done for eight judges

Table 19

Probation Officers--Legal vs. Extra-Legal

Variables--Sample 1-Stage Three

Prob. Officer	R2-Legal Variables	R2--Extra-Legal Variables	Differences
1	.30	.35	.05
2	.40*a	.52*	.12
3	.34*	.39*	.05
4	.28	.31	.03
5	.36*	.37*	.01
6	.26	.41*	.15
7	.24	.30	.06
8	.44*	.50*	.06
9	.30*	.37*	.07
10	.41*	.44*	.03

a
    One asterisk indicates significance at the .05
level. All figures are rounded to two places.

in sample 1. The results are shown in Table 20. A-
gain, one sees a remarkable consistency among the
judges with some variation. The Beta's for RPO, recommendation of probation officer, have the highest
value of the three variables in the analysis for all
eight judges. The signs go in the same direction almost without exception and the magnitudes seem to be
similar. However, there is some variation. For example, X20, pre-trial status, is second in importance
for sample 2 as a whole, but NA, number of arrests, is
second in importance for four judges. The unstandardized path coefficients also show variation. For example, the unstandardized path coefficient for NA,
number of arrests, is -.12 for sample 1 as a whole,
but the unstandardized path coefficents for the eight
judges for NA vary from -.11 to -.85.

A test was performed for the equality of regression coefficients just as it was done for the ten probation officers in sample 1. The full model utilized
all Betas of each judge for each variable as a separate
variable, and the reduced model combined all Beta's for
each judge for each variable into one variable and the

117

results of the full and reduced model were compared. For example, each Beta for NA, number of arrests, for each judge was used as a separate variable for the full model, and all Beta's for all judges for NA were combined into one variable in the reduced model. The results for all variables showed that all coefficients were not significantly different from each other. This proves that judges are consistent among themselves.

Table 20

Standardized, Unstandardized Path Coefficients--

R2--Judges--DJ Dependent Variable--Sample 1-Stage Three

| Judge | N | Independent Variable[a] | | | R2 |
		NA	RPO	X20	
1	91	(-.11) -.33**b	(.40) .43**	(-.17) -.05	.46**
2	60	(-.20) -.09	(.86) .77**	(-.23) (-.10)	.73**
3	47	(.25) .09	(.95) .89**	(-.49) -.02	.78**
4	63	(-.43) -.12	(.64) .57**	(-.41) -.10	.45**
5	49	(-.35) -.18*	(.76) .70**	(-.32) -.17	.72**
6	42	(-.85) -.22	(.33) .29	(-.51) -.28*	.34**
7	63	(-.69) -.003	(.77) .76**	(-.34) .17*	.68**
8	49	(-.12) -.03	(.79)** .79	(-.39) -.17	.75**
Sample 1	979	(-.21) -.09**	(.66) .64**	(-.36) -.17**	.58**

a
See Table 1 for a list of the variables.

b
The unstandardized path coefficients are inside parentheses and the standardized path coefficients are outside the parentheses. One asterisk indicates significance at the .05 level and two asterisks indicate significance at the .01 level. All path coefficients are rounded to two places.

The same type of analysis was done for six judges in sample 2. The results are shown in Table 21. Again, the results show remarkable consistency with some variation. For example, Y22, out of remand, is the strongest factor in sentencing for all six judges. The seriousness of final charge is second in importance, with one exception. The signs go in the same direction, almost without exception. The unstandardized path coefficients show that Y22 has the biggest impact for all six judges. The unstandardized path coefficients vary for SFC, seriousness of final charge, and Y21, remand, from .24 to -.72 for the former and from .00 to .96 for the latter.

Table 21

Standardized, Unstandardized Path Coefficients--

R^2--Judges--DJ Dependent Variable--Sample 2-Stage Three

Judge	Independent Variable			R^2
	SFC	Y21	Y22[a]	
1	(.78)	(.96)	(1.8)	
	.36**b	.16	.66**	.62**
2	(.80)	(.00)	(2.6)	
	.23	.00	.63**	.42**
3	(-.72)	(.46)	(2.9)	
	-.04	.10	.70	.40**
4	(.24)	(-.86)	(2.2)	
	.13	.00	.75**	.63*
5	(.35)	(.66)	(2.2)	
	.23*	.21	.80	.54**
6	(.36)	(.88)	(2.4)	
	.17	.03	.76	.65**
Sample 2[c]	(.40)	(.39)	(2.3)	
	.19**	.09**	.73**	.56**

[a] See Table 1 for a complete list of variables.

[b] One asterisk indicates significance at the .05 level, and two asterisks indicate significance at the .01 level. The unstandardized path coefficients are inside parentheses, and the standardized path coefficients are outside parentheses. All path coefficients are rounded to two places.

[c] The mean number of cases per judge is 44, and the N for sample 2 as a whole is 836.

As in sample 1, a test for the equality of regression coefficients was performed, in the same way as it was performed for the ten probation officers and eight judges in sample 1. For example, the full model for Y22, out of remand, utilized each Beta for each judge for Y22 as a separate variable and the reduced model combined all Betas for Y22 into one variable. The results were analyzed by an F test. None of the regression coefficients was significantly different from each other. This proves that the six judges are consistent.

Another way to test for consistency is to compare the total R^2s of the judges and probation officers in samples 1 and 2 as a whole. Looking at Table 18, the R^2s for probation officers in sample 1 is .30. Looking at Table 20, the R^2 for judges in sample 1 is .58. Looking at Table 21, the R^2 for judges in sample 2 is .56. This shows that judges might be more consistent than probabion officers, because the R^2s of judges are higher than the R^2s of probation officers. There is a lot more unexplained variation for probation officers than for judges. This might be due to the fact that judges depend strongly on recommendation of probation officers in sample 1 and pre-trial status in sample 2. These two factors were found to have a strong influence on disposition of judges.

Summarizing the results of stage three, the test for the equality of regression coefficients proved that both probation officers and judges are consistent, that is, they evaluate similar cases in similar ways. However, the unstandardized path coefficients showed variation among judges and probation officers; judges and probation officers do not place the same emphasis on the same factors. It seems that this variation is partially explained by the method used to test for consistency, because variables which were not important at the group level were excluded at the individual level.

Discriminant Analysis

Discriminant analysis is a statistical technique which distinguishes between two or more groups by forming a linear combination of a set of variables which best differentiates between or among the groups. It is a technique which examines a pattern of weights which gives us a much better account of the nature of group differences than does looking at each variable

separately without regard to their inter-relations.[1]
Discriminant analysis can show results which are different from results of path analysis and these results
may be the true ones. For example, variables which are
not important in path analysis can be important in discriminant analysis, and variables which are important
in path analysis can be unimportant in discriminant analysis. Path analysis assumes equal spacing, a single
scale for the dependent variable, while discriminant
analysis makes no such assumptions. It could be informative, therefore, to compare the results of path analysis to discriminant analysis.

As mentioned previously discriminant scores are
analogous to beta weights in path analysis, and the
percentage of cases correctly classified can be converted into a value analogous to R^2 in path analysis. The
percentage of cases correctly classified can be used to
check the adequacy of the discriminant functions. In
addition, discriminant analysis excludes variables from
the analysis which don't meet certain statistical criteria, and it shows which functions are significant and
which aren't significant. In path analysis, only one
variable at a time is analyzed for significance. Thus,
there are advantages in discriminant analysis compared
to path analysis.

In this section, the results of discriminant analysis for RPO, recommendations of probation officer, and
DJ, disposition of judge in samples 1, 2, and 3 are
presented. These are the key variables in the analysis.
The variable, pre-trial status, is coded as a dichotomy
in this research and, according to Tatsuoka, discriminant analysis for two groups is reduced to multiple regression analysis.[2] In this case, nothing new would be
learned by analyzing pre-trial status, since only one
function would be possible.

As mentioned in Chapter III, discriminant analysis
is a way of discriminating among the several groups on
the basis of several discriminating variables. The

---

[1]Tatsuoka, 5.

[2]Maurice N. Tatsuoka, Multivariate Analysis Techniques for Educational and Psychological Research, New
York: John Wiley and Sons, 1971, 157-93.

discriminant function in standardized form tells the relative contribution of the variables to that function. The variables with the highest weights, ignoring the signs, which only tell whether or not that variable is making a positive or negative contribution to that function, can be used to name the dominant characteristics of that function. The variables associated with that function often express a factor of some importance.[1]

The maximum number of functions is either the number of groups minus one or equal to the number of variables, whichever is smaller. The groups for RPO, recommendation of probation officer, and DJ, disposition of judge, in sample 1, are identical, namely, jail, probation, conditional discharge, fine, and unconditional discharge. Since there are five groups in sample 1 for the two dependent variables, the maximum number of functions is four. In sample 2, probation is excluded. Therefore, there are four groups, namely, jail, conditional discharge, fine, and unconditional discharge. Therefore, three functions are possible for disposition of judge. In sample 3, there are four groups, namely, jail, probation, conditional discharge, and fine. Since there were no cases for unconditional discharge, and only one case for a fine, there are only three groups in sample 3, and two functions are possible for disposition of judge.[2]

However, not all discriminant functions are significant. There are certain methods which are used to determine the importance of the discriminant functions. One way to tell the importance of a discriminant function is by the eigenvalue, a special measure derived in computing the discriminant function. It is a measure of the relative importance of that function. A single eigenvalue is expressed as a percentage of the total sum of eigenvalues and this tells us how important the function is. The sum of the eigenvalues is a measure of the total variation existing in the discriminating variables.[3]

---

[1]Nie et al., Chapter 23.

[2]Jail includes time served and commitment to a drug facility as an in-patient, and probation includes a split sentence.

[3]Nie et al. Chapter 23.

122

Another way of determining the importance of the discriminant function is by the values of the canonical correlation which is the correlation between the discriminant function and the variables which define the group membership. The canonical correlation squared is the proportion of variance in the discriminant function explained by the group. In one way analysis of variance the canonical correlation would be called eta, the correlation ratio.[1]

One test to judge the importance of the discriminant function is Wilks lambda with its transformation into a chi-square statistic for a test of significance. Wilks lambda tests the statistical significance of discriminating information not already accounted for by earlier functions. The larger lambda is, the less discriminating information remains.[2]

The computerized program for discriminant analysis for SPSS doesn't use all the variables put into the analysis. The variables are processed through a stepwise procedure, and they must meet certain criteria to stay in the analysis. The step-wise procedure can be controlled by an "F to enter or to remove" test. The variables which have the highest values according to the selection process are paired with other variables to form sets of best-predicting variables. In this research, any set of variables which shows an F value of one or more, will remain in the analysis, and any variable which falls below one, will be removed from the analysis. One is the default value of the computer program, and any value higher than one can be specified by the researcher.

In addition to the "F to enter or to remove" test, the variables in the analysis are tested further to see if they still make a significant contribution to the analysis. In this research, Rao's V, which is a general distance measure, is used to test the significance of the discriminating variables further. Rao's V is tested for significance by chi-square analysis, and the larger Rao's V, the more discriminating power among the variables. Wilks lambda, in addition to

---

[1] Ibid.

[2] Ibid.

123

determining the importance of the functions, is also used to discriminate among the variables in the analysis. Since the selection process among variables takes place before the functions are derived, the functions will not contain all the variables used in the analysis, since several variables will have been excluded by this selection process.[1]

The discriminant functions can be plotted. However, in order to plot the functions, it is necessary to know the centroids, or group means. Each group has only one centroid, but each group has a different centroid for each function. Therefore, in sample 1, since there are five groups and four functions possible for each of the two dependent variables, there will be 20 centroids printed for both recommendation of probation officer and disposition of judge. In sample 2, since four groups and three functions are possible, there will be twelve centroids printed for disposition of judge. In sample 3, since three groups and two functions are possible, there will be six centroids printed for disposition of judge.[2] However, not all functions are significant.

The discriminant analysis program also prints a classification table which tells the percentage of cases correctly classified for each group. In this way, it is possible to compare the difference between the theoretical and observed scores for each unit in the analysis. It is possible to make a Bayesian adjustment for each group on the basis of prior knowledge of group membership.[3] A Bayesian adjustment for prior group membership is made in this research. Morrison believes that unless this adjustment is made, a bias occurs because of the different sample sizes used to compute the discriminant functions and the classification tables.[4]

It is possible to rotate the discriminant function axes in order to improve the interpretability of the

---

[1]Ibid.

[2]Ibid.

[3]Ibid.

[4]Donald Morrison, "Discriminant Analysis", 446.

axes, since the main variables are highlighted. This is the varimax solution.[1] The varimax solution was performed for all three samples. However, SPSS also prints the unrotated standardized discriminant function coefficients as well as the eigenvalues, relative percentage of eigenvalues, canonical correlations, Wilks lambda chi-square values, and the statistical significance of the chi-square values for Wilks lambda associated with the unrotated functions. SPSS doesn't print these statistics for the rotated functions, but it does show the percentage of variance accounted for by each function, indicating the relative importance of each function.

Sample 1

The relative percentage of eigenvalue for DJ indicated that the first two functions totaled 95.9% or 96%; this means that the first two functions account for 96% of the variance. The canonical correlation showed that the first two functions accounted for most of the variance, .78 for function 1 and .47 for function 2. Wilks lambda showed that the first two functions had the smallest values (the smaller lambda is, the more discriminating power in the function) and that after the first two functions were derived, the value of Wilks lambda was .97. Although the chi-square values showed that all functions were statistically significant, the rotated solution indicated that functions 1 and 2 contribute about 93% to the total variance. Therefore, only functions 1 and 2 are plotted.

The rotated standardized discriminant function coefficients are shown in Table 22. It is necessary to inspect the coefficients of the variables associated with the functions to name the dominant characteristics. Looking at Table 22, function 1, RPO, recommendation of the probation officer, has the highest coefficient. All other coefficients are small. Therefore, function 1 will be called RPO, or recommendation of the probation officer.

Looking at function 2, it can be seen that X20, pre-trial status, has the highest coefficient, with a value of .61. The next highest coefficient is X11, poor adjustment in a prior correctional program, with a value

---

[1]Nie et al., 444.

of .41. The third highest coefficient is NA, number of arrests, with a value of .36. Based on X20, X11 and NA, function 2 will be called pre-trial status--prior record.

The five centroids for functions 1 and 2 are shown in Table 23. In Figure 3, the group centroids are plotted against functions 1 and 2. The group centroids are enclosed in circles corresponding to the five groups.

Table 22

Rotated Standardized Discriminant Function
Coefficients--DJ Dependent Variable-Sample 1

Variable[a]	Function 1[b]	Function 2[b]
RPO	1.00[c]	.01
X20	.05	.61
X11	.11	.41
NA	-.06	.36
X8	.09	.21
SPA	-.19	-.27
X7	.15	.12
X12	-.07	-.22
X19	.03	.10
X21	-.03	.00
SFC	-.00	.05
X4	.04	.03
X5	-.01	.02
X31	.12	.01
X28	.05	-.15

[a]see Table 1 for a complete list of variables.

[b]All values are rounded to two places.

[c]Very often the sign of the coefficients for the rotated functions is the opposite to the sign of the coefficients for the unrotated functions.

126

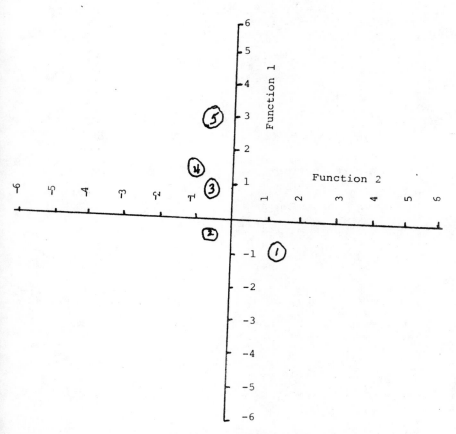

Fig.3. Group centroids Plotted Against Rotated
Discriminant Functions 1 and 2--DJ Dependent
Variable--Sample 1.

127

Table 23

Group Centroids--DJ Dependent Variable

Sample 1

Group	Function 2	Function 2
1	-1.13^{a}	1.41^{a}
2	$-.42$	$-.43$
3	$.97$	$-.51$
4	1.59	$-.79$
5	3.2	$-.62$

[a]These figures are rounded to two places.

Looking at Figure 3, it can be seen that function 1 separates groups 1 and 2 from groups 3, 4 and 5. Function 2 separates group 1 from groups 2, 3, 4 and 5. Group 2 seems somewhat separated from group 1 and group 5 seems somewhat separated from groups 3 and 4. Based on this analysis, it seems that judges take the recommendation of the probation officer into consideration when sentencing a defendant to jail or to probation. The judges also consider the pre-trial status and prior record when sentencing a defendant to jail. Perhaps judges rely on probation officers for the most severe dispositions because they trust their judgment, or perhaps this is a way for judges to shift responsibility to the probation officers. It seems that jail and probation are singled out, possibly because judges know that these are the two most severe dispositions.

The results of discriminant analysis can be compared to the results of path analysis for disposition of judge in sample 1. Path analysis revealed that the recommendation of the probation officer was the most important factor for the disposition of the judge, severe dispositions corresponding to severe recommendations and lenient dispositions corresponding to lenient recommendations. Discriminant analysis also revealed that the recommendation of the probation officer was the most important factor which discriminated among the dispositions because it was associated with the most important function. However, in addition, discriminant analysis revealed that judges rely heavily on the recommendation of the probation officer for the most severe dispositions, namely jail and probation.

Path analysis revealed that pre-trial status was the second greatest factor for the disposition of the judge, with those in remand receiving more severe dispositions. Path analysis also revealed that the number of arrests was the third most important factor for the disposition of the judge, with the greater number of arrests associated with the more severe dispositions. Path analysis revealed that a poor adjustment in a prior correctional program only had an indirect effect on disposition of the judge, with a poor adjustment associated with severe dispositions. In discriminant analysis, pre-trial status, number of arrests, and poor adjustment in a prior correctional program, all legal variables were associated with the second strongest function, but these variables were most important for the disposition of jail.

It is possible to calculate an R^2 analogous to R^2 in path analysis by use of a statistic called proportion of reduction in errors. It is calculated in the following way:

$$\text{P.R.E.} = \frac{\text{\# errors (random) - \# errors (DA)}}{\text{\# errors (random)}}[1]$$

which indicates that the proportion of reduction of errors is equal to the number of errors based on chance minus the number of errors based on discriminanat analysis divided by the number of errors based on chance. The result, the P.R.E., is the R^2 based on discriminant analysis. Calculating the P.R.E. in this way, the R^2 in discriminant analysis was .64 compared to the R^2 of .58 in path analysis (see Table 15). In other words, discriminant analysis has reduced the number of errors by 64% over a strictly random or chance basis. The proportion of variance explained is .64, which is higher than the .58 in path analysis. Discriminant analysis

---

[1]Herman J. Loether and Donald G. McTavish, Descriptive Statistics for Sociologists--An Introduction, Boston: Allyn and Bacon, Inc., 1974, 212-20.

usually explains more variance than path analysis does for the same data. The percentage of cases correctly classified by discriminant analysis was 75.28%.

One can see both similarities and differences between path analysis and discriminant analysis.

Recommendation of probation officer, RPO, as dependent variable will now be analyzed. The relative percentage of eigenvalues for unrotated functions 1 and 2 is 91%, and the canonical correlation is highest for functions 1 and 2. In addition, Wilks lambda shows the lowest value for functions 1 and 2 (the lower Wilks lambda, the more discriminating power to that function). However, the chi-square test for Wilks lambda shows that functions 1, 2 and 3 are significant but function 4 is not significant. The rotated functions show that function 1 accounts for about 73% of the variance, function 2 for about 13% of the variance, function 3 for about 8% of the variance, and function 4 for about 5-1/2% of the variance. Since the unrotated functions show that functions 1, 2 and 3 are significant, only functions 1, 2 and 3 are plotted and analyzed.

The rotated standardized discriminant function coefficients are presented in Table 24. Looking at Table 24, it can be seen that the highest values for function 1 are NA, number of arrests, X20, pre-trial status, and X11, poor adjustment in a prior correctional program. Again, function 1 will be called pre-trial status--prior record. Looking at function 2, it can be seen that the highest values are X3, age under 10, X8, no promises, and SPA, seriousness of prior arrests. These are both legal and extra-legal variables. However, promises are not necessarily legal variables. Based on X3 and X8, function 2 will be called extra-legal variables. Looking at function 3, it can be seen that X31, the interaction of Black defendant and employment, X12, good adjustment in a prior correctional program, and X6, employment, show the highest values. Again these are both legal and extra-legal variables. Based on X31 and X6, function 3 will be called employment.

The group means or centroids for the three functions are shown in Table 25. The group centroids are plotted against the functions.

Functions 1 and 2 are plotted in Figure 4. It seems that function 1 separates group 1 from groups 2, 3, 4 and 5. Function 2 separates groups 3, 4 and 5 from groups 1 and 2. However, groups 3, 4 and 5 are

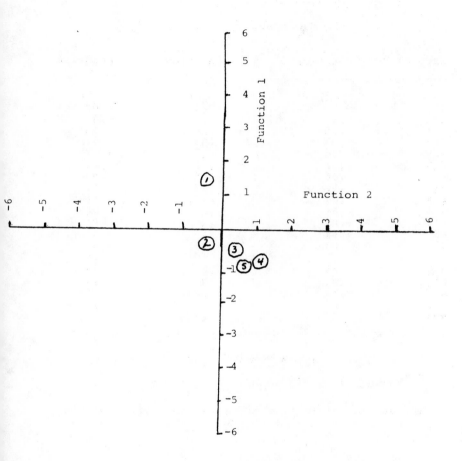

Fig. 4.   Group Centroids Plotted Against Rotated Discriminant
           Functions 1 and 2.   RPO Dependent Variable--Sample 1.

131

Table 24

Rotated Standardized Discriminant Function Coefficients

RPQ Dependent Variable--Sample 1

Variable[a]	Function 1	Function 2	Function 3
	[b]	[b]	[b]
NA	.57	-.26	-.09
X20	.53	.00	-.05
X11	.49	.20	.16
X29	-.31	.00	.03
X26	.25	-.01	-.17
X28	-.22	.21	.14
X3	.09	-.55	-.05
X8	.16	.47	.31
SPA	.04	.43	-.14
X31	-.04	.06	.66
X12	-.09	.09	.59
X6	-.08	.29	-.54
X2	.03	.08	-.35
X7	.03.	.32	.35
SFC	.03	-.01	-.34
X5	.03	.07	-.24
X4	-.02	-.07	.05
X21	.02	-.09	.23
X30	-.02	.16	-.09

[a] see Table 1 for a complete list of variables.

[b] These values are rounded to two places.

hardly separated at all. Groups 1 and 2 are somewhat
separated but group 2 is not separated very much from
groups 3, 4 and 5.

Functions 1 and 3 are plotted in Figure 5. It
seems that group 1 is separated the most from all the
other groups. Function 1 separates group 1 from
groups 2, 3, 4 and5. Groups 2, 3, 4 and 5 are hardly
separated at all. However, function 2 does separate
groups 1 and 3 from groups 2, 4 and 5.

Functions 2 and 3 are plotted in Figure 6. It
seems that none of the groups is separated very much
from the other groups. However, function 2 does

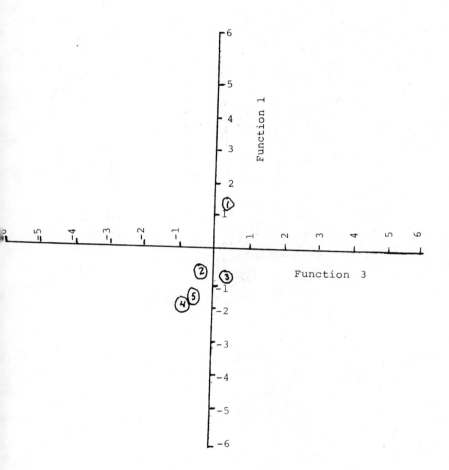

Fig. 5. Group Centroids Plotted Against Rotated
Discrimant Functions 1 and 3--RPO Dependent
Variable--Sample 1.

133

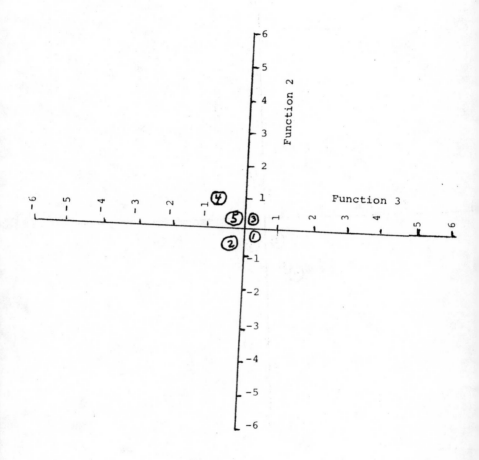

Fig. 6.   Group Centroids Plotted Against Rotated
Discriminant Functions 2 and 3--RPO Dependent
Variable--Sample 1.

Table 25

Group Centroids--RPO Dependent Variable

Sample 1

Group	Function 1	Function 2	Function 3
	[a]	[a]	[a]
1	1.47	-.14	.27
2	- .33	-.32	- .11
3	- .50	.36	.09
4	- .68	.91	-1.12
5	- .78	.51	- .71

[a]These values are rounded to two places.

separate groups 3, 4 and 5 from groups 1 and 2 and function 3 does separate groups 1 and 3 from groups 2, 4 and 5. Group 4 seems a little more separated from the rest of the groups.

Summarizing, it seems that probation officers recommend jail on the basis of pre-trial status and prior record of the defendant. It seems that jail is singled out here from all the other dispositions. Jail was also singled out in analyzing the dispositions of the judges in sample 1. Perhaps judges and probation officers believe that since jail is the most severe disposition, special consideration should be given to a defendant's case before he is sentenced to jail.

Functions 2 and 3 didn't separate the groups very well. Perhaps probation officers consider extra-legal factors for all dispositions. However, one should not underestimate the importance of extra-legal variables. This researcher has seen many probation officers go to great lengths to verify employment and age. Employment can very often mean the difference between probation and a conditional discharge.

The interaction term X31, Black defendant and employment, was associated with function 3. It is difficult to say if probation officers are discriminating because of this. First, Blacks who are employed may get preferential treatment. Second, Puerto Ricans are not necessarily discriminated against. Third, employment

135

was also associated with function 2, and the values for
X30, X31, the racial categories, were very low. Fourth,
this analysis has not revealed any evidence of discrimination for other variables, e.g., ethnicity of the defendant, victim, offender-victim category. It is possible that since Blacks constitute the largest ethnic
group, probation officers unconsciously or consciously
associate employment with this group.

It is possible to compare the results of discriminant analysis to the results of path analysis for recommendation of probation officer. In path analysis, number of arrests, pre-trial status, and poor adjustment in
a prior correctional program showed the strongest effects on recommendation of probation officers. All
these paths had a negative effect on recommendation,
that is, the more the defendant was arrested, was in
remand, or had a poor adjustment in a prior correctional program, the more severe the recommendation. In
discriminant analysis, these three variables were associated with the strongest function; however, in addition,
discriminant analysis revealed that these variables were
most important for the recommendation of jail only.

Path analysis revealed that the extra-legal variables, age and employment each only explained about 2%
of the variance. The addition of age and employment
only added 3% to the total R^2, or proportion of variance explained, indicating the importance of legal
variables. Discriminant analysis revealed that the
extra-legal variables were associated mainly with the
weakest functions. Discriminant analysis also revealed that the extra-legal variables didn't separate
the groups very much, indicating that possibly probation officers use extra-legal variables for all dispositions. However, based on observation, it was revealed that one should not underestimate the importance
of extra-legal variables, which can sometimes mean the
difference between a severe or lenient disposition.

Discriminant analysis revealed the importance of
the variable X31, interaction of Black defendant and
employment for function 3. Path analysis didn't reveal this variable as a factor for recommendation (see
Table 15).

Just as for DJ, disposition of judge, it is possible to obtain an R^2 analogous to R^2 in path analysis
by means of a proportion of reduction in error measure.
This measure revealed an R^2 of .39 compared to an R^2 of

.30 in path analysis (see Table 15). This means that the variables in discriminant analysis explained about 40% of the variance. This is higher than path analysis. The percentage of cases correctly classified by discriminant analysis was 57.9%

It seems that a comparison between the results of path analysis to the results of discriminant analysis has revealed both similarities and differences.

Sample 2

Discriminant analysis was also performed for sample 2, for DJ, disposition of the judge. The relative percentage of eigenvalues for unrotated functions 1 and 2 is 99%. The canonical correlations for unrotated functions 1 and 2 are .81 and .43 respectively. Wilks lambda shows the smallest values for functions 1 and 2 (the smaller Wilks lambda, the more that function discriminates among the variables.) The chi-square test of significance for Wilks lambda shows that only functions 1 and 2 are significant. The rotated functions show that function 1 accounts for 85.39% of the variance, function 2 accounts for 9.56% of the variance, and function 3 accounts for 5.05% of the variance. Therefore, only functions 1 and 2 will be analyzed.

The rotated standardized discriminant function coefficients for DJ, disposition of judge in sample 2, are shown in Table 26. Looking at function 1, it can be seen that Y22, out of remand, has the highest value. Based on Y22, function 1 will be called pre-trial status. Looking at function 2, it can be seen that SOC, seriousness of original charge has the highest value. Therefore, function 2 will be called SOC, seriousness of original charge.

The four centroids for functions 1 and 2 are shown in Table 27. Functions 1 and 2 are plotted in Figure 7. It can be seen that jail is separated strongly from the other groups. Function 1 separates group 1 from groups 3, 4 and 5. Function 2 separates group 4 from groups 1, 3 and 5. Groups 3, 4 and 5 are not separated very well. It seems that jail is singled out on the basis of pre-trial status. It seems that jail, conditional and unconditionsl discharge are separated on the basis of the original charge. Judges in sample 2 sentence a defendant to jail on the basis of pre-trial status and to jail, conditional and unconditional discharge on the

137

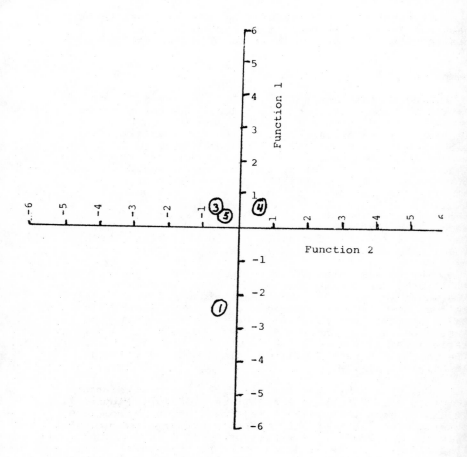

Fig. 7. Group Centroids Plotted Against Rotated
Discriminant Functions 1 and 2--DJ Dependent
Variable--Sample 2.

Table 26

Rotated Standardized Discriminant Function

Coefficients--DJ Dependent Variable

Sample 2

Variable[a]	Function 1[b]	Function 2[b]
Y22	1.02	.01
Y24	.16	.00
SOC	- .09	.73
Y10	- .12	.40
Y5	.06	.31
Y4	- .02	-.30
NA	- .21	.24
Y18	- .04	-.21
Y9	.04	-.20
Y15	- .07	.19
SFC	.06	-.09
Y20	- .00	.10
Y14	.10	-.02
SPA	.04	.07
Y21	.07	-.07
Y17	- .06	-.07
Y16	- .05	-.11
Y25	.09	-.15

[a]see Table 1 for a complete list of variables.

[b]All values are rounded to two places.

basis of seriousness of original charge.

The results of discriminant analysis can be compared
to the results of path analysis for sample 2. In path
analysis, Y22, or pre-trial status, was the most important
factor for the disposition of the judge, with those out of
remand receiving lenient dispositions and and those in remand receiving more severe dispositions. In discriminant
analysis, pre-trial status was associated with the strongest function; however, discriminant analysis revealed that
pre-trial status separated jail from the other dispositions.
Judges sentence a defendant to jail on the basis of pre-
trial status. Path analysis revealed that the seriousness

Table 27

Group Centroids--DJ Dependent
Variable--Sample 2

Group	Function 1	Function 2
	-2.62 [a]	-.23 [a]
1	-2.62	-.23
3	.64	-.49
4	.72	.48
5	.54	-.52

[a] All figures are rounded to two places

of the final charge was the second most important factor
for disposition of judge, with more serious final charges
associated with more severe dispositions and less serious
final charges associated with more lenient dispositions.
Seriousness of final charge was not important in discriminant analysis. However, discriminant analysis revealed that seriousness of original charge separated
fines from jail, conditional and unconditional discharge.
In path analysis, seriousness of original charge only
had an indirect effect on disposition of judge (see
Table 16).

Just as in sample 1, a P.R.E., or proportion of reduction in error measure was calculated to give an R^2 in
discriminant analysis comparable to the R^2 in path analysis. The results showed an R^2 of .55 which is just about
equal to the R^2 of .56 in path analysis (see Table 16).
The percentage of cases correctly classified in discriminant analysis was 70.45%.

One can see the similarities and differences between the results of path analysis and discriminant analysis. One again can see the importance of pre-trial status for the disposition of the judge.

Sample 3

Discriminant analysis was performed for DJ, disposition of judge, in sample 3. Here, there were only

140

three groups, jail, probation and conditional discharge, since the disposition of fine only had one case and there were no cases for unconditional discharge. Since there were only three groups, only two functions are possible. The unrotated functions revealed that function 1 accounted for 68.54% of the relative percentage of eigenvalues and function 2 accounted for 31.46% of the eigenvalues. The canonical correlations for the unrotated functions were .47 for function 1 and .34 for function 2. The Wilks lambda revealed that function 1 was the stronger of the two functions (the higher Wilks lambda, the less discriminating power). However, the significance test for Wilks lambda revealed that only function 1 was significant; the significance level for function 2 was .07. The rotated functions revealed that function 1 accounted for about 58% of the variance and function 2 for about 42% of the variance. Since the statistics revealed that both functions have a great deal of discriminatory power, both functions are plotted.

The standardized discriminant function coefficients for functions 1 and 2 are shown in Table 28. The highest value is Z3, age under 19. The second highest value is SPA, seriousness of prior arrests. The third highest value is Z6, warrants. The fourth highest value is Z5, promises. The fifth highest value is Z9, Puerto Rican complainant. This function includes both legal and extra-legal variables. However, based on seriousness of prior arrests, promises and warrants, function 1 will be called prior record. Looking at function 2, NA, number of arrests, has the highest value, and Z4, sex, the second highest value. Based on NA, function 2 will be called arrests.

The three group centroids for functions 1 and 2 are shown in Table 29. The group centroids are plotted against functions 1 and 2 in Figure 8. It seems that group 3 is separated from groups 1 and 2. Function 1 clearly separates group 3 from groups 1 and 2, and function 2 separates group 1 from groups 2 and 3. Group 1 is somewhat separated from group 2. It seems that judges will sentence a defendant to a lenient disposition, conditionsl discharge, on the basis of prior record. It also seems that judges will not release a defendant to the streets without considering the arrest record, because practically all the defendants in sample 3 are in remand. It has also been stated that sample 3 has the most serious prior record (see Table 6). This again confirms the importance of pre-trial status, since about 99% of the defendants in sample 3 are in remand.

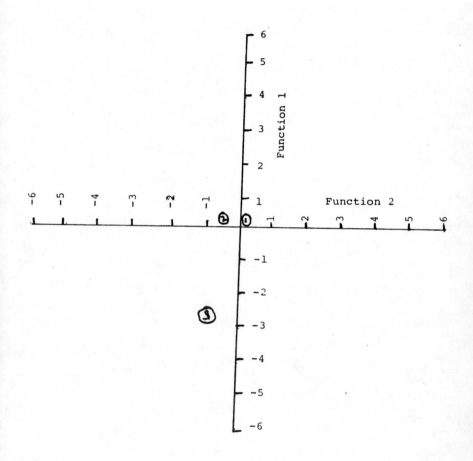

Fig. 8.   Group Centroids Plotted Against Rotated
          Discriminant Functions 1 and 2--DJ Dependent
          Variable-Sample 3.

Table 28

Rotated Standardized Discriminant Function

Coefficients--DJ Dependent Variable

Sample 3

Variable[a]	Function 1	Function 2
	[b]	[b]
Z3	.66	-.13
SPA	-.56	-.10
Z6	.46	-.36
Z5	.45	.07
Z9	.40	-.21
NA	.16	.75
Z4	.05	.50

[a] see Table 1 for a complete list of variables.

[b] All figures are rounded to two places.

Perhaps judges know that most of the defendants in sample 3 will get a jail sentence because of a bargain made with the district attorney, and that is why judges are not as concerned about jail as about probation and conditional discharge, dispositions which will mean releasing the defendant at the time of sentencing.

Comparing the results of discriminant analysis to path analysis in sample 3, path analysis revealed that the number of arrests was the strongest factor associated with sentencing, with more arrests associated with severe dispositions. Path analysis revealed that seriousness of prior arrests had only an indirect effect. Path analysis revealed that the number of arrests only explained about 8% of the variance (see Table 17). Discriminant analysis revealed the importance of seriousness of prior arrests and number of arrests, as well as prior record, for example, warrants, promises. Discriminant analysis also revealed that probation and conditional discharge were separated from jail by the number of arrests and that conditional discharge was separated from probation and jail by prior record.

Table 29

Group Centroids--DJ Dependent Variable

Sample 3

Group	Function 1	Function 2
	.08[a]	.21[a]
1	.08	.21
2	.30	-.80
3	-2.10	-.87

[a]All values are rounded to two places.

Just as in samples 1 and 2, a P.R.E., or proportion
of reduction in error measure was calculated and the results showed an R^2 of .45 which is higher than the R^2 of
.08 in path analysis. Discriminanat analysis revealed
that 80.81% of the cases were classified correctly.

There are both similarities and differences between
the results of path analysis and discriminant analysis.
One again can see the importance of pre-trial status and
prior record.

Summary

The findings have been presented in this chapter.
The defendants are mainly Black and Puerto Rican, male,
over 19, and unmarried. About half are employed or in
school. The defendants are charged mainly with property
crimes in samples 1 and 3 but most of the charges are
victimless in sample 2. Sample 2 has the lightest prior
record and sample 3 the heaviest. It was found that
judges follow the recommendation of the probation officer most of the time. It was found that sample 2 received
the most lenient dispositions, e.g., fines most frequently, and sample 3 the most severe dispositions, e.g., jail
most frequently. Sample 1 was in-between, receiving probation most frequently. For jail sentences in Class A
misdemeanors, sample 2 received the most lenient dispositions, and sample 3 the most severe dispositions, with
sample 1 in-between. Sample 2 received more lenient

fines compared to sample 1.

The results of path analysis were presented. Path analysis was performed in three stages. Stage one involved analyzing all paths which directly affected the dependent variables in the full model except those excluded on the basis of theoretical perspectives. Stage two involved eliminating all paths which either failed to meet statistical significance on at least a .05 level or failed to obtain magnitudes of at least + .10. Stage 3 involved analyzing the individual paths of a sample of judges and probation officers.

The results showed that judges rely heavily on the recommendations of the probation officer. The legal variables were very important for both judges and probation officers in sample 1 and judges in samples 1 and 2; number of arrests and poor adjustment in a prior correctional program were very important for probation officers in sample 1; seriousness of final charge was very important for judges in sample 2, and the number of arrests was very important for judges in sample 3. Variables influenced outcomes both directly and indirectly.

Judges and probation officers showed remarkable consistency with some variation in their sentencing outcomes.

The results of discriminant analysis showed both similarities and differences compared to the results of path analysis. Some of the similarities showed that the recommendations of probation officers and the legal variables were very important. Some of the differences showed that jail is separated from the other dispositions on the basis of pre-trial status and prior record both for judges and probation officers in sample 1. Another difference showed that judges in sample 3 release a defendant to the street on the basis of number of arrests, and that judges give a conditional discharge on the basis of prior record. Another difference showed that in sample 2, jail is separated from the other dispositions on the basis of pre-trial status, and seriousness of original charge separates jail, conditional and unconditional discharge from a fine. Discriminant analysis showed that extra-legal variables didn't separate the groups very well, perhaps indicating that probation officers consider extra-legal variables for all dispositions. However, their importance is emphasized.

145

The eight research questions posed in Chapter II will be presented and answered in light of the findings of this research. The conclusions and limitations of the study wi also be presented.

Chapter V

CONCLUSIONS, IMPLICATIONS,

LIMITATIONS

Based on the findings of this research, it is now
possible to answer the eight research questions posed
in Chapter II. The eight questions will be presented
and answered in the order in which they appeared in
Chapter II. There will be a general discussion of the
implications of the findings, and some limitations on
the present research will be presented.

Questions Posed and Answered
1. What factors do judges use in their sentencing dispositions?

Both path analysis and discriminant analysis revealed that the recommendation of the probation officer was the strongest factor for the disposition of judges in sample 1. Path analysis revealed that the total
effect of this factor on the disposition of the judge
explained about 44% of the variance. Discriminant analysis revealed that the recommendation of the probation
officer was associated with the strongest function.
However, discriminant analysis also revealed that the
recommendation of the probation officer was most important for the most severe dispositions, namely, jail
and probation. It seems that judges rely heavily on
probation officers, especially for the most severe
dispositions. Perhaps judges believe that incarcerat-
ing a defendant or placing him on probation is a grave
responsibility for which they would rather share responsibility. Perhaps they rely on the professional
judgment of the probation officer. This research cannot answer why judges depend on probation officers in
sentencing decisions.

Path analysis revealed that judges in sample 1
consider the pre-trial status of the defendant next in
importance to recommendations for sentencing dispositions. The direct effect on disposition explained
about 13% of the variance. More severe dispositions
are associated with remand and less severe dispositions are associated with not being in remand. Perhaps judges believe that once a defendant is in remand,
he ought to stay there. Perhaps judges are influenced

147

negatively by remand, or perhaps they negotiate with prosecutors to sentence a certain percentage of defendants in
remand to severe dispositions. Here, the selection process for remand is crucial. Perhaps defendants in remand are handicapped by lack of resources, e.g., time,
money, legal services, etc., to fight their cases.
Again, the data cannot explain why judges are influenced
by pre-trial status of the defendant.

Path analysis revealed that the number of arrests
was the third most important factor for the disposition
of the judge in sample 1. The direct effect explained
less than 1% of the variance, but the total effect explained about 13-1/2% of the variance. The greater
the number of arrests, the more severe the disposition,
and the less the number of arrests, the more lenient
the disposition. This certainly is not surprising, because this finding is revealed in the review of the
literature. It seems logical that judges are influenced
by a norm in which the prior record of the defendant is
a factor in sentencing. The recidivism factor is crucial in evaluating criminal justice output.

Discriminant analysis in sample 1 revealed that
legal factors were associated with the second most important function.

Discriminant analysis also revealed that jail was
separated from the other dispositions on the basis of
legal factors, pre-trial status, poor adjustment in a
prior correctional program, and number of arrests. It
seems that judges will sentence a defendant to jail on
the basis of several factors.

Path analysis in sample 1 also revealed that many
factors had indirect effects only on disposition of
the judge. Each indirect effect explained from less
than 1% of the variance to about 8% of the variance.
Seriousness of prior arrests had an indirect effect,
with less serious prior arrests associated with less
severe dispositions. Warrants also had an indirect
effect, with more warrants associated with more severe
dispositions. A poor adjustment in a prior correctional program meant more severe dispositions. In addition,
the number of arrests and seriousness of final charge
interacted with a poor adjustment to produce a more severe disposition. Promises interacted with pre-trial
status, or remand, to produce a more severe disposition.
Again, one sees the influence of legal variables affecting the sentencing process.

However, non-legal variables had indirect effects. Both age and the offender-victim category of Black, Puerto Rican defendant versus White complainant each explained less than 1% of the variance, and hence were unimportant. Legal aid indirectly explained about 7% of the variance, with more severe dispositions associated with legal aid. Perhaps legal aid does not defend as vigorously as private counsel. However, the relation between legal aid and disposition might be spurious, because legal aid might only defend certain types of defendants. The interaction variable of White defendant and employment indirectly explained about 3% of the variance with more lenient dispositions associated with this category. It is difficult to say if judges discriminate, because the indirect effect is very low.

In sample 2, pre-trial status or out of remand showed the greatest direct effect in path analysis for the disposition of the judge. Those who were out of remand received the most lenient dispositions compared to those who were in remand. Discriminant analysis also revealed that pre-trial status was associated with the strongest function, but that it was most important for the disposition of jail. Again, one sees the importance of pre-trial status but one cannot answer from an analysis of the data why judges consider this an important factor in sentencing.

Path analysis also revealed in sample 2 that seriousness of final charge was second in importance for the disposition of the judge. The total effect explained about 13% of the variance. The more severe final charges were associated with more severe dispositions and more lenient final charges were associated with more lenient dispositions. Discriminant analysis didn't reveal that seriousness of final charge was important, but did reveal that seriousness of original charge separated jail, conditionsl and unconditional discharge from a fine. Judges sentence defendants to jail, a conditional and an unconditional discharge on the basis of original charge.

Path analysis also revealed the indirect effect of several variables in sample 2. The indirect effects explained separately from less than 1% of the variance to about 13% of the variance. The legal variables revealed that the more the number of warrants, the more severe the disposition of the judge. The less serious the prior arrests, and the more lenient the disposition of prior convictions, the more lenient the disposition of the judge.

The indirect effects of the extra-legal variables were mainly in the ethnic categories. The more the defendant was Black, the more lenient the disposition of the judge. The offender-victim categories of White versus White, Black, Puerto Rican versus White, and Black, Puerto Rican versus Black, Puerto Rican, were all associated with more severe dispositions, but each explained from less than 1% of the variace to about 2-1/2% of the variance. Legal aid was associated with more severe dispositions, again perhaps indicating that they do not defend as vigorously as private counsel.

In sample 3, path analysis revealed that the greater the number of arrests, the more severe the disposition of the judge. Discriminant analysis revealed that legal variables are associated with the more lenient dispositions, namely, probation and conditional discharge, indicating that judges are reluctant to release a defendant to the street without careful consideration since virtually all defendants in sample 3 are in remand.

It seems that judges sentence defendants mainly on the basis of legal variables, pre-trial status, number of arrests, adjustment in a prior correctional program, seriousness of original and final charge, seriousness of prior arrests, disposition of prior conviction, etc. All factors are not weighed equally, however. Some, like pre-trial status and number of arrests, had greater effects than others. Some, like disposition of prior convictions, only had indirect effects. It seems that the prior record of the defendant is important. The probation officers' recommendations are very important in sample 1, especially for the more severe dispositions of jail and probation. It seems that jail and probation are singled out, perhaps indicating that judges believe that these dispositions require careful consideration because they are the most severe dispositions.

It seems that a probation report can be a key to a more severe disposition. Defendants who are sentenced without a probation report have more chance of receiving a lighter sentence, possibly due to the less serious original and final charges, and the pre-trial status of the defendant. It was also found that defendants in sample 2 have lighter prior records compared to defendants in samples 1 and 3.

There is no evidence of racial discrimination in

sentencing dispositions. First, the category of Black defendant and the category of White defendant and employment, both revealed more lenient dispositions, and each had only indirect effects. Second, three offender-victim categories were involved in more severe dispositions and each explained from less than 1% of the variance to about 2-1/2% of the variance, and had only indirect effects. Third, discriminant analysis revealed the unimportance of ethnic categories.

2. What factors do probation officers use in their sentencing recommendations?

The results of path analysis revealed that the number of arrests had the greatest direct effect on recommendation of probation officers. The total effect explained about 12% of the variance. The more the number of arrests, the more severe the recommendation. This is in agreement with Langerman who concluded that the number of arrests was the most important factor affecting recommendations of the probation officers.[1]

Pre-trial status had the second greatest direct effect on recommendations, with a total effect of -.42, explaining about 18% of the variance. The more the defendant is in remand, the more severe the recommendation of the probation officer. Again, it can be seen how pre-trial status affects decisions of probation officers. Just like judges, perhaps they believe that once a defendant is in remand, he ought to stay in jail.

The third greatest direct effect on recommendation was a poor adjustment in a prior correctional program, with a total effect of -.30, explaining 9% of the variance. The more a defendant made a poor adjustment in either parole, probation or a drug program, the more severe the recommendation.

Discriminant analysis revealed that the number of arrests, pre-trial status and poor adjustment in a prior correctional program were associated with the strongest function. Therefore, the results of discriminant analysis agree with the results of path analysis in this respect. However, discriminant analysis revealed that the legal variables were very important for the recommendation of jail only. It seems that probation officers recommend jail, the most severe disposition, on the basis of several legal variables. It was stated in question 1 that discriminant analysis had

---

[1]Langerman.

revealed that judges sentence a defendant to jail on the basis of probation officers' recommendations which in turn are influenced directly by legal factors. Perhaps one reason why judges trust the recommendation of probation officers for severe dispositions is because they are aware of the factors probation officers use in recommending jail.

Path analysis also revealed the direct influence of several other legal factors in recommendations. One of these factors was seriousness of prior arrests, with less serious prior arrests associated with less severe recommendations. The number of arrests and seriousness of final charge meant a more severe recommendation for those with a poor adjustment in a prior correctional program, and more lenient recommendation for those with a good adjustment in a prior correctional program. This indicates interaction among the variables, adjustment in a prior correctional program, number of arrests, and seriousness of final charge. The total effect of seriousness of prior arrests and the two interaction terns each explained from less than 1% of the variance to about 8% of the variance.

In addition, several factors had indirect effects only on recommendations. Promises interacted with remand to produce more severe recommendations. Sex, the offender victim category of Black, Puerto Rican defendant versus White complainant, and the interaction variable of White defendant and employment each explained less than 1% of the variance. More warrants meant more severe recommendations, and less warrants meant more lenient recommendation. Greater use of legal aid meant more severe recommendations. One reason, perhaps, as suggested by Blumberg, is that legal aid is coopted into becoming an agent to help the defendant redefine his situation and his perceptions consistent with pleading guilty.[1] If this is true, legal aid would be used as an important agent to maintain guilty pleas, rather than used to help defendants in their sentencing outcomes. Perhaps this is why legal aid lawyers don't try to influence probation officers, because the officers are not influential in obtaining pleas.

---

[1]Abraham S. Blumberg, "The Practice of Law as a Confidence Game, Organizational Cooption of a Profession", Law and Society Review, June, 1967, 1:15-39.

Extra-legal variables directly affected recommendations. Age showed that youthful offenders were given
more severe recommendations, but the total effect explained about 1% of the variance. The other extra-legal
variable, employment, showed that more lenient recommendations were associated with employment, or staying
in school. However, a step-wise procedure revealed that
the extra-legal variables of age and employment only
contributed 3% to the total R^2, thus emphasizing the
importance of legal variables, prior record.

However, discriminant analysis revealed that extra-
legal variables didn't separate any groups very well.
Perhaps this indicates that probation officers consider extra-legal variables for all dispositions. Although
discriminant analysis revealed the unimportance of
extra-legal variables compared to legal variables, observation by the researcher revealed that extra-legal
variables can be decisive, for example, can mean the
difference between probation and a conditional discharge.

There is no evidence of racial discrimination in
probation officers' recommendations. First, path
analysis revealed that ethnic categories had small, .
indirect effects only, explaining less than 1% of the
variance. Second, discriminant analysis revealed that
two racial categories, X2, Black defendant and X30,
White defendant and employment, had very low values.
Third, the interaction term, X31, Black defendant and
employment, had a high coefficient, but was associated
with the weakest function in the analysis, and employment itself was associated with a stronger function
which was not associated with race. It is possible
for Blacks who are employed to receive preferential
recommendations.

One again sees the importance of legal variables
and prior record in probation officers' recommendations.
It seems that probation officers single out jail compared to the other dispositions. In question 1, it was
revealed that judges single out jail and probation compared to the other dispositions. Perhaps severe dispositions are signled out for serious consideration. Although legal variables are important for recommendations,
one should not underestimate the importance of extra-
legal variables such as employment, which can be a decisive factor in recommendations.

It seems that several factors have a small impact
on recommendations. Not all factors, however, are
equally important for recommendations. The factor of

employment for consideration of dispositions seems logical in light of the consensus that employment or staying in school is justified as a prognosis in criminal
justice. It is believed in our society that employment
or staying in school will prevent crime or is a rehabilitative measure against crime. Perhaps there is some
degree of truth in this, but the empirical evidence is
contradictory; for example, white-collar crime. Probation officers inculcate some of society's value systems, and since probation is associated with rehabilitation, it is logical to assume that being employed or
staying in school is a prime step in rehabilitation.
Employment as a factor in recommending a fine seems
logical, because a fine can sometimes be paid more
with a defendant who is employed than with one who is
unemployed or on public welfare.

3. Do judges follow probation officers' recommendations? To what extent?

The findings indicated that in identical cases,
judges follow the recommendations of the probation officers in 793 cases out of 979 cases, or 81% of the
time. In cases of disagreement, the judges are more
punitive in 106 cases, or 57% of the time, and less
punitive in 80 cases, or 43% of the time. This difference is statistically significant.

Both path analysis and discriminant analysis revealed that the recommendation of the probation officer
was the most important factor for disposition of the
judge. There was a positive correlation, that is,
severe recommendations were associated with severe
dispositions and lenient recommendations were associated with lenient dispositions. The recommendations of
probation officers were very important for the two most
severe dispositions, namely, jail and probation.

It seems that the probation officers are seen as
a very important agent at Brooklyn Criminal Court, and
the judges rely heavily on their recommendations, especially for severe sentences. However, another explanation is that probation officers recommend what they
know or believe that the judges want to hear, and that is
why their recommendations are followed so much by the
judges. It is difficult to tell from the data why judges follow probation officers' recommendations; any
reasons would be logical guesses open to empirical investigation.

4.   Is there a set of regularities that judges
      and probation officers follow in their
      sentencing dispositions and recommendations?

One way to determine this empirically is by looking
at the total R^2 of probation officers and judges in all
three samples. Explained variation can be equated with
orderliness, regularities, and unexplained variation with
randomness. The total R^2 for probation officers in
sample 1 was .30, and the R^2 for probation officers in
discriminant analysis was .39. The R^2 for judges in
sample 2 was .56 in path analysis and .55 in discriminant analysis. The R^2 for judges in sample 3 was .08
in path analysis, and the R^2 was .45 in discriminant
analysis.   The R^2 for judges in sample 1 was .58 and
.64.

The above analysis indicates that for probation
officers, there is a lot of randomness. Path analysis
also revealed a lot of randomness for judges in sample
3, but discriminant analysis revealed a much higher R^2
for judges in sample 3. Therefore, generally, judges
seem to show a much higher R^2 compared to probation
officers, possibly due to the influence of one or two
factors, e.g, recommendation of probation officers,
pre-trial status, legal variables. This perhaps indicates that judges adhere to regularities more than
probation officers.

However, the analysis and findings have revealed
that judges and probation officers adhere to a number
of regularities in the sentencing process. These factors were repeatedly found important and they can be
stated as generalizations:

a.   Judges rely heavily on the recommendation
of the probation officer for disposition, particularly for jail and probation.

b.   Three of the most important legal variables
for both dispositions and recommendations are
the number of arrests, pre-trial status and prior
adjustment in a correctional program. The greater the number of arrests, the more the defendant
is in remand, and the more the defendant's adjustment in a prior correctional program is
poor, the more severe both the recommendations
of the probation officer and disposition of
the judge. On the other hand, the less the
number of arrests, the less the defendant is
in remand, and the better the adjustment in

a prior correctional program, the more
lenient the recommendation and disposition. No prior arrests can often, but
not always, mean an unconditional discharge, which is the least severe disposition. Being out of remand and charged
with non-serious crime can mean a
lenient disposition.

Moreover, there is interaction. The number of
arrests and seriousness of final charge can mean a
more severe disposition to a defendant with a poor adjustment in a prior correctional program, and can mean
a more lenient disposition to a defendant with a good
adjusment in a prior correctional program. A promise
by the district attorney can interact indirectly with
remand to produce a more severe disposition.

    c.   The more severe dispositions seem to
be singled out. Jail and probation are singled
out on the basis of the recommendation of
the probation officer and jail is singled
out on the basis of pre-trial status and
prior record, perhaps indicating that serious
consideration is given to severe dispositions.

    d.   Both the seriousness of the original
charge and the seriousness of final charge
are important in dispositions. A non-serious
charge, for example, a victimless charge,
will usually result in a defendant being
sentenced without a probation report. If a
defendant is out of remand and charged with
a non-serious crime, sentenced without a
probation report, his most severe disposition
will be a conditional discharge. The seriousness of final charge has a great effect on
disposition of judge. Defendants sentenced
without a probation report usually have
lighter prior records and receive lighter
dispositions compared to defendants sentenced
with a probation report. A less serious
original charge may result in lenient dispositions without a probation report.

It seems that a key factor to a severe disposition
is the recommendation of the probation officer. A key
factor in whether or not a defendant receives a probation report is the seriousness of final charge. Some
of the legal actors revealed to this researcher that
very often the prior record of the defendants is not
investigated in cases of sentencing without a

probation report due to time factors. This researcher
noticed the absence of many prior records for defendants
sentenced without a probation report.

It seems that the seriousness of the final charge
reflects our society's value system. Victimless crimes
are considered non-serious in our society. Crimes
against property and persons are considered much more
serious, and both legal and social punishments are
stronger here compared to victimless crimes. A crime
against property, for example, petit larceny, will very
often result in a severe disposition compared to a crime
like public intoxication.

e.   Extra-legal variables affect the sentencing
decisions. Although extra-legal factors are
less important than legal factors they do affect sentencing outcomes. Extra-legal factors
affect every sentencing recommendation of the
probation officer. Employment, and school, are
particularly important for the recommendation
of probation. It seems that probation officers
reflect our society's value system and the normative consensus that employment or staying in
school are justified as prognosis in criminal
justice rehabilitation.

Where do judges and probation officers learn these
regularities? Hoane suggests that social values per-
petuated in our society carry over to the plea-bargaining
process.[1] The pilot study conducted by this researcher
indicated that judges and probation officers interact
among themselves and with other legal actors; perhaps
this is where they learn the regularities. However,
the matter is far from settled and as Langerman suggests,
more research is needed to find out where probation officers learn to abide by the regularities.[2]

5.   Are judges consistent in their sentencing
practices?

Consistency is defined as the handling of similar
cases in similar ways or equal sentences for equal
cases. Consistency was tested empirically by comparing
the paths of individual judges in samples 1 and 2 to

---

[1]Hoane.

[2]Langerman, 3.

157

the paths of samples 1 and 2 as a whole. Based on the magnitudes of the Beta coefficients and signs judges show remarkable consistency with some variation in both samples 1 and 2. In addition, a test for the equality of regression coefficients indicated that judges are highly consistent in both samples.

One can ask if the sentence a defendant receives depends on the particular judge assigned to his case. The answer is both yes and no. Although judges are consistent, there is some variation, which means that some judges do not stick strictly to the regularities in sentencing. In addition, there is a lot of unexplained variation, which can mean that some defendants can receive a disposition which depends on a particular judge assigned to the case.

6.   Are probation officers consistent in their sentencing recommendations?

The same kind of analysis which was performed for judges was performed for probation officers. The results showed remarkable consistency among the probation officers with some variation. The test for equality of regression coefficients also revealed that probation officers were consistent. A step-wise procedure performed for each probation officer separately revealed that legal factors have a greater impact in sentencing than non-legal factors for every probation officer in the analysis.

Again, one can ask if the sentence a defendant receives depends on the particular probation officer assigned to the case. Just as for judges, the answer is again both yes and no. Probation officers are consistent; they evaluate similar cases in similar ways. To a great extent it doesn't matter which probation officer is assigned to the case, because the results will probably turn out to be the same. However, there is some variation and a lot of unexplained variation. This unexplained variation can mean that probation officers take unique factors into account in the sentencing process. To a certain extent, then, the sentence which the defendant receives depends on the particular probation officer assigned to the case.

As mentioned previously, in both path analysis and discriminant analysis, the R^2s of the judges for samples 1 and 2 and in discriminant analysis the R^2 of the judges in sample 3 seem to be higher than the R^2 of the

probation officers in sample 1. This can mean that
judges are more consistent than probation officers, although both judges and probation officers are consistent. This is due to the fact that recommendations of
probation officers in sample 1, pre-trial status in sample
2, and legal variables in sample 3, have a great impact on
the sentencing decisions. There is no one particular factor that has an analogous impact on recommendation of
probation officer. However, there is a lot of unexplained
variation and, therefore, it is difficult to say whether
judges or probation officers are the more consistent.

      7.   Do defendants receive individual atten-
      tion in the disposition of their cases?

    It is difficult to define and to operationalize
individual attention. Individual attention in this research means the attempt and efforts made by probation
officers and judges to ascertain the particular problems
and needs of each defendant in order to impose the proper sentence. For example, if a defendant is suffering
from a drug problem, a probation officer or judge will
see that referral is made to the proper correctional
program. The time spent on a particular case sometimes
can and sometimes cannot be indicative of individual
attention. As mentioned in Chapter II, if probation
officers and judges abide by regularities, it is possible, but not definite, that individual attention can
suffer.

    It has already been mentioned that the total R^2s
of probation officers and judges don't explain every-
thing; there is a lot of unexplained variation. This
researcher believes that a good part of this randomness
is due to the individual attention that probation officers and judges give to each case.

    The pilot study in which this researcher conducted
interviews with probation officers and judges revealed
that they very often gave individual attention to each
case. This researcher's power of observation can verify this. This researcher has seen many probation officers try to lecture and admonish defendants to re-
frain from being arrested; he has seen many probation
officers go to great lengths to try to help defendants
by trying to get them into a drug or alcoholic program,
referring them to employment, etc. Very often there is
a great deal of empathy between probation officers and
defendants, even though a defendant is still under investigation by the court and hasn't been sentenced yet.

Very often a probation officer will go to extremes to
get an evaluation from a correctional agency and will
adjourn cases pending a psychiatric examination. Many
probation officers will go to great lengths to talk to
relatives, mothers, wives or friends. All these things
can directly or indirectly mean a suitable sentence for
a defendant; for example, probation instead of jail.

Although this researcher has not observed judges
directly, there are some indicators that they too give
individual attention to cases. They very often adjourn
cases to evaluate the progress of a defendant in a drug
program or other program, in which defendants are
placed by the court before sentencing. They very often
adjourn cases pending a psychiatric evaluation by the
court. They very often adjourn cases at the request
of the probation officer because more information is
needed. All these things can affect sentencing, although the consequences of the outcomes are difficult
to predict.

Another indicator of individual attention is the
proportion of variance explained by extra-legal variables. This research revealed that most of the variance explained was due to legal variables; extra-
legal variables only added about 3% to the total R^2 in
sample 1, and extra-leval variables only added a maximum of 15% to the R^2 of each individual probation officer. However, only two variables were considered,
age and employment. Other variables not in the analysis might explain individual attention to defendants'
cases.

It is difficult to say whether or not defendants
who are sentenced without a probation report in sample
2 receive less, more or the same amount of attention as
defendants in sample 1 who are sentenced with a probation report. The R^2 in path analysis for judges in
sample 1 was .58 and in sample 2 was .56. In sample 3,
the R^2 for judges was .08. This might indicate that
judges give the same amount of attention to cases in
samples 1 and 2 and more attention in sample 3, but it
is difficult to say for certain because unexplained
variation can mean either variables not bought into the
analysis or subjective factors, or both. The R^2 for
probation officers was .30 in sample 1, but it is difficult to say that probation officers give more attention to defendants than judges because of the unknown
factors in the unexplained variation.

8. Who influences the sentencing process?

This research has revealed that judges share power with probation officers. The recommendations of probation officers have a great deal of weight in sentencing decisions. Other actors, too, share in the sentencing decisions. In the pilot study conducted by this researcher among prosecutors and legal aid lawyers, it was revealed that they, too, influence the sentencing decisions.

The recommendation of the district attorney is usually recorded in the court papers. Promises as a variable were found unimportant in this research. However, promises were recorded as dichotomy, indicating the absence or presence of a promise, not the actual promise itself. A review of the content of the promises revealed that the promises were loosely constructed with several alternatives, very flexible. For example, a promise would very often have a minimum and maximum term or a recommendation of two sentencing dispositions.[1] The vagueness of the promise, in this researcher's opinion, strengthens the conclusion that sentencing is shared and not restricted to one or two legal actors.

It is also possible that a complainant or a police officer can be the key factors in a sentencing decision. A relative can also have a lot of influence. The defendant himself, for example, by cooperating in a drug progran, can sometimes influence his own sentence.

Discussion

One of the most important conclusions of this research is that the probation officer's role is very important in sentencing at Brooklyn Criminal Court. Judges rely heavily on probation officers for sentencing, especially for the severe dispositions of jail and probation. Probation officers constantly verify the number of arrests, a variable found important in sentencing. They constantly evauate adjustment in a

---

[1]The vagueness of the promises is relative to time and place. In some jurisdictions, promises were quite definite. Presently, the evidence indicates more definite promises at Brooklyn Criminal Court.

prior correctional program, another important variable. They contact significant others in the defendants' lives and these significant others very often figure in the sentencing decisions. They counsel defendants and refer them to programs, factors which directly or indirectly figure in the sentencing decisions. They use both subjective and objective factors in making a recommendation.

Sentencing is a grave responsibility. Perhaps judges believe that sentencing decisions should be shared; this would alleviate a great deal of responsibility from the judges' shoulders. On the other hand, judges share responsibility with legal aid lawyers and prosecutors, although their influence was not studied in this research. Very often, judges have praised probation officers, both for a fine report and an intelligent recommendation; however, many judges have criticized probation officers for failing to include all the important facts necessary to make an intelligent recommendation, or failing to make an intelligent recommendation. Judges at times will not hesitate to criticize probation officers publicly in court or to mention the probation officer's recommendation publicly to the defendant. This can indicate the importance of the probation officer in the judge's opinion. Judges very often confer with probation officers.

Some critics have argued that the probation officer's role can be eliminated from the system without serious consequences. A report on probation in New York City revealed that judges who relied on heavily on promises followed the recommendation of the probation officers in about 8% of the cases, thus questioning the importance of the probation officer's role.[1] Langerman has questioned the role of the probation officer.[2] Robison et al. have concluded that judges can come to the same conclusions without probation officers' recommmendations. The influence of probation officers is

---

[1]A Report of the New York City Board of Corrections, "Pre-Sentence Reports--Utility or Futility", Fordham Urban Law Journal, 1973-4, 2:27-56.

[2]Langerman, 26.

[3]James Robison, Leslie Wilkins, Robert Carter and Albert Wahl, San Francisco Project--A Study of Federal Probation and Parole, San Francisco: Institute of Mental Health, 1964.

relative to time and place. However, in spite of this, this researcher believes that the role of the probation officer is functional to the organization of Brooklyn Criminal Court, although the consequences of probation officers' actions are sometimes difficult to anticipate. This supports the organizational perspective.

Another important conclusion is that certain key variables affect the sentencing decisions. These key variables are number of arrests, adjustment in prior correctional program, pre-trial status, and seriousness of final charge. These are legal variables. Certainly this finding is not new. A review of the literature reveals that number of arrests figures in sentencing dispositions.[1] Many researchers have found evidence that defendants in remand receive unfavorable dispositions. The seriousness of original and final charges is an important factor in many sentencing studies. Although adjustment in a prior correctional program is not used often as a variable in research, it seems logical that defendants who do poorly on parole or probation would get a more severe disposition compared to defendants who do well on parole or probation.

The point is that a defendant's prior record follows him in the sentencing process. Pre-trial status, for example, is influenced by number of arrests, adjustment in a prior correctional program, warrants, seriousness of charge, disposition of prior convictions, etc. (See Tables 15 and 16.) Although not studied here, adjustment on prior correctional program can be influenced by the number of arrests. Rate of rearrest is a key factor in evaluating any correctional program. The seriousness of final charge determines whether or not a defendant will be sentenced with or without a probation report, and a probation report can be a key to a more severe disposition.

In other words, the sentence a defendant receives can be predicted to a certain extent. If a defendant is charged with a victimless crime, and is sentenced without a probation report, he will probably receive a lenient sentence. If a defendant has a great number of arrests, the sentence he receives will depend on

---

[1]Green found that the number of arrests had no influence in sentencing. See Green, _Judicial Attitudes in Sentencing_.

whether or not he is in remand. However, remand will depend to a great extent on number of arrests, prior record, seriousness of charge, adjustment in correctional program, etc. The research has revealed some interaction between adjustment in prior correctional program, number of arrests, and seriousness of final charge. Although not all interaction has been studied, and some interaction was eliminated due to multicollinearity, the four key variables directly or indirectly influence both each other and sentencing outcomes.

Other factors not brought into the analysis might be very important. Pre-trial status, for exmaple, might be determined by prosecution's recommendations, community ties of the defendant, etc. One factor suggested is that defendants in remand give an animal-like appearance and this might consciously or unconsciously affect both probation officers and judges in their sentencing decisions.[1] Plea-bargaining might determine the seriousness of final charge.

Although legal variables were found more important than non-legal variables, these latter variables do have some effect. Particularly important is employment. Both probation officers and judges are directly and indirectly influenced by this factor. Even if all the odds are against the defendant, this factor can be decisive for the defendant's fate. Defendants who are employed or in school have a better chance of receiving a favorable disposition compared to those who are unemployed or out of school. As mentioned previously, this reflects our society's value system. Judges and probation officers inculcate these value systems into their sentencing decision. There is logic to this, because there is an economic basis for crime. Very often, defendants will commit crimes to survive economically. Probation officers and judges will sometimes place defendants into training programs and will base their sentencing decisions on the defendants' attitudes toward these programs.

Another important conclusion of this research is that there is no basis to conclude that judges and probation officers are discriminatory in their sentencing practices. Although occasionally a racial category

1   John Irwin, lecture delivered for the course "Administration of Justice", New York University, New York, April, 1974.

appeared in the findings, it was not strong enough to conclude discrimination in sentencing. Perhaps one reason is that most defendants, regardless of race, are in the lower SES classes, and therefore, there is no reason to discriminate. However, this research cannot answer the question fully, because there are many subjective factors that can affect sentencing, in the relationship between a defendant and a probation officer, for example, which can be based on discriminatory factors. However, based on objective factors there is no evidence of racial discrimination. Therefore, it is concluded that there is no support for the conflict theory.

Another important conclusion is that probation officers and judges rely on regularities because these make the sentencing process logical and orderly. If judges and probation officers didn't depend on recommendation, legal variables, employment, seriousness of final charge, sentencing might be chaotic and random. These regularities act as pivot points in which sentencing is seen as a rational, logical, and coherent process. These regularities don't have to be questioned in order to depend on them for sentencing. That is, if a defendant is in pre-trial remand or has a great number of arrests, the probation officer or judge doesn't have to question why a defendant is in remand or why he has a heavy record; the objective facts can be taken as criteria for sentencing decisions. This, however, doesn't mean that probation officers never probe for reasons for negative factors. Many probation officers have revealed that they have stayed up late at night in some cases in order to come to a proper recommendation. This dependence on regularities simply means that the objective factors can be taken on face value as predictors for outcomes.

There is a lot of unexplained variation. The unexplained variation can be the result of both objective and subjective factors. This research has revealed that defendants do receive a great deal of individual attention in some cases. Although probation officers and judges are consistent, there is a great deal of discretion in their decisions. Sentencing is not a completely objective process. If it were, perhaps computers could do the sentencing. To a certain, unmeasured extent, the sentence a defendant receives depends on the particular judge and probation officer assigned to the case.

In summary, it is concluded that sentencing at Brooklyn Criminal Court, a misdemeanor court, is not a completely mechanical, routinized, uniform process. It is a complicated process, based on both objective and subjective factors. There are many key elements which go into the sentencing process, for example, probation officers' recommendations, district attorney's recommendations, legal and extra-legal variables, subjective factors, etc. Sentencing, in this researcher's opinion, could not be a completely routinized process because of the discretionary aspects of the criminal justice system.

This study might have implications for the legal institutions of the larger society. Since judges depend so heavily on probation officers, perhaps probation officers could do the sentencing and judges could devote their time to other aspects of the criminal justice system, such as determination of guilt or innocence. There is nothing inevitable about judges sentencing offenders in misdemeanor courts. A review of the literature has revealed that judges should be aided by experts in the field of human behavior, such as psychology, sociology, social work, etc.

The fact that this research has failed to reveal any discrimination might mean that the influx of Black judges into our courts, the increased expansion of education, the political movements and racial riots of the 1960's and 1970's, the legal protection of minority groups, etc. have all interacted to reduce discrimination in our legal institutions.

Limitations

This research, as other research, suffers from limitations. First, this study was confined to one court in one borough, and empirical investigation must determine if the criteria are applicable to other courts in New York City, as well as in other cities.

A second limitation is that not enough relevant variables were included in the research, such as type of conviction, degree of premeditation, and remorse of the defendant, legal evidence, subjective evaluation of the probation officer, attitudes on punishment, interaction terms, etc. This is true of other research also.

A third limitation applies to the scaling of the

variables. One can question whether the variables, seriousness of prior arrests, seriousness of original and final charge, and disposition of prior convictions were scaled properly. Perhaps not enough relevant information was obtained to code and scale these variables, for example, assessment of personal injury and amount of damage.

However, one must be practical in doing research, and factors of time, money, and expediency are limitations on any research. Although more variables might have increased the explanatory power of the research, other factors, such as power analysis, could counterbalance this, e.g., too many variables could cut the power of the significance tests. Variables should not be included in research unless there are reasons for doing so.

This researcher believes, however, that important variables as revealed in the review of the literature and based on two pilot studies, were included in this research.

A summary of this research is presented in Chapter VI.

Chapter VI

SUMMARY

This research is a study of the sentencing practices of judges and the recommendations of probation officers at Brooklyn Criminal Court located at 120 Schermerhorn Street, Brooklyn. This researcher is a probation officer, assigned to Brooklyn Criminal Court's Investigation Division, who received special permission to do the study. This is one of the few studies confined to New York City and to a lower criminal court, where the caseloads consist mainly of misdemeanors and a small percentage of violations.[1]

The cases were selected for the years January 1, 1972 through June 30, 1975 and from April 1, 1976, through December 31, 1976. The research years were from July 1, 1976 through September, 1978.

Three random samples were selected from closed probation cases and court papers. Sample 1 consisted of a systematic sample of 983 cases in which defendants were sentenced with a probation report. Sample 2 consisted of a systematic sample of 836 cases in which defendants were sentenced without a probation report. Sample 3 consisted of a systematic sample of 100 cases in which the defendants were mainly in jail or received jail as a disposition, and in which the probation officer prepared a short report without either verification or a recommendation.

Two pilot studies were conducted to determine the important variables and the scaling of some of the variables. The first pilot study consisted of interviews with judges, probation officers, legal aid lawyers, and district attorneys. Many of the same variables found important as a result of this pilot study were the same ones found important in the review

---

[1]Violations by law carry a maximum penalty of 15 days jail, one year probation, or a fine.

of the literature, e.g., number of arrests, number of convictions, seriousness of original and final charge, type of conviction, ties in the community, injury to the complainant. Many but not all of the important variables were selected for inclusion in the research.

The second pilot study was a content analysis of the probation cases to determine reasons given by probation officers for a specific recommendation. This researcher decided against using these "reasons" as findings because they can represent rationalizations rather than true reasons. Many, but not all of the "reasons" were included as variables in this research.

The quantitative methods used were path analysis and discriminant analysis. A combination of both dummy variables and variables measured on an interval level were used in the analysis. Several variables were eliminated from all three samples due to multicollinearity. Observation supplemented quantitative analysis.

Path analysis was performed in three stages. Stage one consisted of performing a path analysis on all the dependent variables excluding the multicollinear variables and variables excluded by theoretical perspectives. The dependent variables in sample 1 were disposition of judge, recommendation of probation officer, and pre-trial status. The dependent variables in sample 2 were pre-trial status and disposition of judge. The dependent variable in sample 3 was disposition of judge. This was the full model.

Stage two of path analysis consisted of deleting all paths which failed to meet two criteria. All paths which failed to obtain significance on at least the .05 level and failed to obtain magnitudes of at least ±.10 were deleted, with a few exceptions. This reduced model consisted of fewer paths than the full model.

Stage three of path analysis consisted of comparing the individual paths of ten probation officers, eight judges in sample 1, and six judges in sample 2, to the paths of the two samples as a whole. This was to empirically test for consistency in sentencing among probation officers and judges.

A test for the equality of regression coefficients

revealed that none of the coefficients in a set of
dummy variables was significantly different from each
other. A test for the equality of regression coefficients also revealed that both probation officers and
judges were consistent in sentencing dispositions.

Discriminant analysis was performed for recommendation of probation officer in sample 1 and disposition of judge in samples 1, 2, and 3.

This research was posed in a series of eight
questions based on conflict theory, discrimination,
and organizational theory. The following are the
research questions posed and answered based on the
results of both the quantitative and qualitative
analysis.

1. What factors do judges use in their sentencing
   dispositions?

Judges base their dispositions very strongly on
the recommendations of the probation officer, especially for the dispositions of jail and probation.
Judges also base their dispositions on legal variables,
namely, pre-trial status, number of arrests, adjustment in a prior correctional program, seriousness of
final charge, seriousness of prior arrest, etc. The
defendants in remand, and the defendants who have a
great number of arrests, receive more severe dispositions. Seriousness of original and final charge are
important for defendants sentenced without a probation
report, in which more lenient charges are associated
with more lenient dispositions. Some variables have
indirect effects only on dispositions.

2. What factors do probation officers use in their
   sentencing recommendations?

The legal variables have the strongest effect on
recommendations. The three legal variables which had
the strongest effect were number of arrests, poor
adjustment in prior correctional program, and pre-
trial status, with poor adjustment, remand, and more
arrests associated with more severe dispositions.
There was some interaction. Some variables had indirect effects only. Probation officers recommend jail
on the basis of pre-trial status and prior record.
Although extra-legal variables were less important
than legal variables, they can be decisive for every
type of recommendation. Many factors had a small
impact on sentencing outcomes.

3. Do judges follow probation officers' recommendations? To what extent?

A comparison of disposition of judge and recommendation of probation officer controlled for case revealed that judges follow probation officers in 81% of the cases. The judges were more punitive in 57% of the cases and less punitive in 43% of the cases compared to probation officers. This difference was statistically significant. Both path analysis and discriminant analysis revealed that judges follow strongly the recommendation of probation officers for sentencing dispositions. Therefore, it is concluded that judges follow probation officers with remarkable consistency.

4. Are there a set of regularities that judges and probation officers follow in their sentencing dispositions and recommendations?

Although the R^2s of the judges and probation officers revealed a lot of unexplained variation, it was concluded that judges and probation officers depend on regularities in their sentencing dispositions. Such regularities were dependence on probation officers' recommendations, dependence on legal variables, dependence on seriousness of final charge for a sentence without a probation report, and use of extra-legal variables. It was concluded that the use of these regularities functions as an order-regulating mechanism and helps to create logic in sentencing. However, discretion is not completely eliminated from the sentencing process.

5. Are judges consistent in their sentencing practices?

The results of stage three of path analysis revealed that judges are remarkably consistent in their sentencing dispositions with some variation. This was based on the magnitudes and signs of the path coefficients for individual judges and the test for equality of regression coefficients.

6. Are probation officers consistent in their sentencing recommendations?

The results of stage three of path analysis revealed that probation officers, like the judges, are remarkably consistent in their recommendations with

172

some variation. This is based on the magnitudes and signs of the path coefficients for individual probation officers as well as the test for equality of regression coefficients.

Although both judges and probation officers are consistent, the sentence a defendant receives depends to a certain extent on the particular probation officer and judge assigned to the case. This is revealed by the proportion of variance unexplained in the analysis.

7. Do defendants receive individual attention in the disposition of their cases?

Based both on the fact that there is a lot of unexplained variation and on observation it was concluded that defendants very often receive a lot of individual attention by judges and probation officers in the disposition of their cases.

8. Who influences the sentencing process?

Since judges rely on the recommendation of the probation officer to a great extent, it was concluded that judges and probation officers share in the sentencing decisions. The pilot study involving interviews with other legal actors also revealed that they too share in the sentencing decisions. This supports an organizational perspective.

One of the most important conclusions of the research was that the probation officer was seen as functional to the working of Brooklyn Criminal Court. The conclusions negated any doubt about the importance of the role of the probation officer in Brooklyn Criminal Court.

Another important conclusion was that there was no evidence of racial discrimination in the sentencing process, thus failing to support the conflict theory.

Another important conclusion was that sentencing can be predicted to a certain extent, because certain key variables are important in the sentencing process. A defendant's prior record, for example, number of arrests and adjustment on prior correctional program, are important.

Another important conclusion was that employment

and school were seen by judges and probation officers as an important value system in our society. Judges and probation officers as criminal justice agents inculcate these values because there is some truth that employment or school are important for rehabilitation.

It was finally concluded that sentencing was a complicated process based on many factors, and not a mechanical, routine mechanism. This research also implied that probation officers might do the sentencing in misdemeanor courts, and that lack of evidence of discrimination might be due to the greater political, legal, and educational rights of minority groups.

This research ended with some limitations. The applicability of the findings outside of Brooklyn and New York City, the inclusion of all relevant variables, and the scaling of the variables were seen as three limitations.

BIBLIOGRAPHY

Asher, Herbert B. Causal Modeling--Quantitative Ap-
plications in the Social Sciences. Beverly Hills:
Sage Company, 1975.

Banfield, Laura and Anderson, David, "Continuances in
the Cook County Criminal Courts," University of
Chicago Law Review, 1968, 35: 259-316.

Beals, Robert L; "Presentence Reports--Allegations of
Prior Criminal Activity--Factual Determination of
Degree of Burden of Proof," Ohio State Law Jour-
nal, 1972, 37: 960-71.

Bing, Stephen R. and Rosenfield, Stephen. The Lower
Criminal Courts of Metropolitan Boston. Boston:
Lawyers Committee for Civil Rights Under Law,
1970.

Blalock, Hubert M. Jr. Causal Models in the Social
Sciences. New York: Aldine Company, 1971.

_____. Social Statistics. Second Edition. New York:
McGraw-Hill, 1972, 325, 515.

Blumberg, Abraham. Criminal Justice. Chicago: Quadran-
gle Books, 1967.

_____; "The Practice of Law as a Confidence Game--
Organizational Cooption of a Profession," Law and
Society Review, June, 1967, 15-39.

Boyle, Richard F; "Path Analysis and Ordinal Data,"
American JOurnal of Sociology, January, 1970, 75:
461-80.

Bruce, Andrew A., et al. The Workings of the Indeterminate Sentence--Law and Parole Systems in Illinois. Montclair: Patterson Smity, 1968, 54.

Bryan, Joseph G: "The Generalized Discriminant Function: Mathematical Foundation and Computational
Routine," Harvard Educational Review, 1951, 21:
90-95.

Bullock, Henry Allen, "Significance of the Racial
    Factor in Length of Prison Sentence," Journal of
    Criminal Law, Criminology and Police Science,
    1961 52: 411-17.

Burke, Peter and Turke, Austin, "Factors Affecting
    Post Arrest Dispositions," Social Problems, 1975,
    22: 313-32.

Campbell, Rutherford B; "Sentencing--The Use of Psych-
    iatric Information for Presentence Reports," Ken-
    tucky Law Journal, 1971, 2, 60: 285-321.

Carter, Robert M. and Wilkins, Leslie T; "Some Factors
    in Sentencing Policy," Journal of Criminal Law,
    Criminology and Police Science, 1967, 58: 503-514.

Chatterje, Samprit and Price, Bertram. Regression
    Analysis by Example. New York: New York University
    Press, 1957, 56-8, 66-8.

Chiricos, Theodore G. and Waldo, Gordon P; "Reply to
    Greenberg, Hopkins, and Reasons," American Socio-
    logical Review, February, 1977, 42: 181-85.

_____; "Socioeconomic Status and Criminal Sentenc-
    ing--An Empirical Assessment of a Conflict Propo-
    sition, American Sociological Review, December,
    1975, 40: 753-72.

Cohen, Jacob and Cohen, Patricia. Applied Multiple
    Regression/Correlation Analysis for the Bahavioral
    Sciences. New York: John Wiley and Sons, 1975,
    9-10, 54-6, 131-2, 152.

Cohen, Jacob. Statistical Power Analysis for the
    Behavioral Sciences. New York: Academic Press,
    1969.

Conklin, John E. Robbery and the Criminal Justice
    System. New York: J.B. Lippincott, 1972, 20.

Davis, Kenneth Culp. Discretionary Justice--A Prelim-
    inary Inquiry. Baton Rouge: Louisiana State Uni-
    versity Press, 1969.

Eisenstein, James and Jacob, Herbert. Felony Justice--
    An Organizational Analysis of Criminal Courts.
    Boston: Little, Brown and Company, 1977.

176

_____, "Sentencing and Other Sanctions in the Criminal Courts of Baltimore, Chicago, and Detroit," Political Science Quarterly, December, 1975, 90: 617-37.

Eldefonso, Edward. Issues In Corrections. Beverly Hills: Glencoe Press, 1974, 18.

Farraro, Thomas. Mathematical Sociology: An Introduction to Fundamentals. New York, John Wiley, 1973, 465-76.

Frank, Jerome. Courts on Trial--Myth and Reality in American Justice. Princeton: Princeton University Press, 1949.

Frankel, Marvin. Criminal Sentences--Law Without Order. New York: Hill and Wang, 1972.

Garfinkel, Harold, "Research Note--Inter and Intra-Racial Homicide, Social Forces, 1949, 27: 369-81.

Gaudet, Frederick. "Individual Differences in Some Sentencing Tendencies of Judges," In Glendon Schubert. Judicial Behavior--a Reader. Chicago: Rand and McNally, 1965, 352-66.

Gaylin, Willard. Partial Justice--A Study of Bargain Sentencing. New York: Alfred A. Knopf, 1974.

Green, Edward, "Inter- and Intra-Racial Crime Relative to Sentencing," Journal of Criminal Law, Criminology, 1964, 55: 348-58.

_____. Judicial Attitudes in Sentencing--A Study of the Factors Underlying the Sentencing Practices of the Criminal Court in Philadelphia. New York: MacMillan Company, 1961.

Hagan, John, "Extra Legal Attributes and Criminal Sanctions--An Assessment of a Sociological Viewpoint," Law and Society Review, 1974, 8: 357-83.

_____, "Law, Order, and Sentencing, A Study of Attitudes in Action," Social Problems, 1975, 38: 374-84.

_____, "The Social and Legal Construction of Criminal Justice--A Survey of Pre-Sentence Process," Social Problems, 1975, 22: 620-32.

Hanushek, Eric A. and Jackson, John E. Statistical Methods for Social Scientists. New York: Academic Press, 1977, 141-3.

Herman, Lawrence. The Right to Counsel in Misdemeanor Court. Columbus: Ohio State Unviersity Press, 1973.

Hinderlang, Michael, "Equality Under the Law," in Jack L. Kuykendall and Charles Reasons. Race, Crime and Justice. Pacific Pallasades: Goodyear Publishing Company, 1972, 318-19, 321.

Hoane, Joseph, "Strategem and Values--An Analysis of Plea Barbaining in an Urban Criminal Court," Unpublished dissertation for the Ph.D., New York University, 1978.

Hogarth, John. Sentencing as a Human Process. Toronto: University of Toronto Press, 1971.

Hopkins, Andrew, "Is There a Class Bias in Sentencing," American Sociological Review, December, 1975, 42: 176-77.

Inlay, Carl H., "The ProbationOfficer--Sentencing and the Winds of Change," Federal Probation, December, 1975, 9-17.

Inciardi, James A., "The Impact of Pre-Sentence Procedures on Subsequent Sentencing," a Paper presented to the 71st annual meeting of the American Sociological Association, 1976, mimeographed.

Irwin, John, lecture delivered for the course, "Administration of Justice," New York University, New York, April, 1974.

Jaris, Dean and Mendelsohn, Robert, "The Judicial Role and Sentencing," Midwest Journal of Political Science, 11: 1967, 471-88.

Johnson, Elmer H., "Selected Factors in Capital Punishment," Social Forces, 1957, 36-156-9.

Johnson, Guy B; "The Negro and Crime," Annals, 217: 93-104.

Johnson, J. Econometric Methods. Second Edition. New York: McGraw-Hill, 1972, 160.

Judson, Charles et al., "A Study of the California Penalty Jury in First Degree Murder Cases," Stanford Law Review, 1969, 21: 1297-1497.

Katz, Lewis R. et al. Justice is the Crime, Pre-Trial Delay in Felony Cases. Cleveland: Press of Case Western University, 1971, 151, 207.

Kerlinger, Fred and Pedhazar, Elazan J. Multiple Regression in Behavioral Research. New York: Holt, Rinehart and Winston, 1973, 305-314.

Kuykendall, Jack L. and Reasons, Charles. Race, Crime and Justice. Pacific Pallasades. Goodyear Publishing Company, 1972, 318-319.

Lackenbruck, Peter A. Discriminant Analysis. New York: Hofner Press, 1975.

Land, Kenneth, "Path Models of Functional Theories of Stratification," Sociological Quarterly, Fall, 1970, 11: 474-484.

Langerman, Herbert, "Determinants of Probation Officers' Pre-Sentence Recommendations," unpublished dissertation for the Ph.D, New York University, New York, 1976.

Levine, Martin A. Urban Politics and the Criminal Courts. Chicago: University of Chicago Press, 1977.

_____; "Urban Politics and Judicial Behavior," Journal of Legal Studies, 1972, 1: 193-221.

Lizotte, Alan J., "Extra-Legal Factors in Chicago's Criminal Courts--Testing the Conflict Model of Criminal Justice," Social Problems, June, 1978, 25: 564-80.

Loether, Herman J. and McTavish, Donald G. Descriptive Statistics for Sociologists--An Introduction. Boston: Allyn and Bacon, Inc., 1974, 212-20.

179

Long, Lucinda. "Innovation in Urban Criminal Courts,"
in Herbert, Jacob, Potential for Reform in
Criminal Justice. Beverly Hills: Sage Publication,
1974, 173.

Karl Marx and Frederick Engels. Selected Works. New
York: International Publishers, 1968, 243.

McCloo, Robert J., "Criminal Procedure--Accuracy of
Presentence Reports," Wayne Law Review, March,
1976, 22 899-912.

McIntyre, Donald, "A Study of Judicial Dominance of
the Charging Process," Journal of Criminal Law,
Criminology and Police Science, December, 1968,
59: 463-90.

Mileski, Maureen, "Courtroom Encounters--An Observation of a Lower Criminal Court," Law and Society
Review, 1971, 51: 473-538.

Mohr, Lawrence B., "Organizations, Decisions, and
Courts," Law and Society Review, Summer, 1976, 10:
621-42.

Morris, Frank L. "The Outsider in the Courtroom--An
Alternative Role for Defense," in Herbert Jacob.
Potential for Reform in Criminal Justice. Beverly
Hills: Sage Publications, 1974, 303.

Morrison, Denton E. and Hankel, R.E. The Significance
Test Controversy--A Reader. Chicago: Aldine, 1970.

Morrison, Donald G., "Discriminant Analysis," in
Robert Ferber. Handbook of Marketing Research.
New York: McGraw-Hill, 1974.

Morse, Wayne and Beattie, Raymond. "A Study of the
Variances in Sentencing Imposed by Circuit Judges,"
in James Klenoski and Robert Mendelsohn. The
Politics of Social Justice. Boston: Little, Brown
and Company, 1970, 176-86.

Mueller, Gerhard G.W. Sentencing--Process and Purpose.
Springfield: Charles C. Thomas, 1977.

Nagel, Stuart, "Disparities in Criminal Procedure,"
University of California Law Review, August, 1967,
14: 1272-1305.

Nagle, Stuart, "Disparities in Criminal Procedure,"
     University of California Law Review, August 1967,
     14: 1272-1305.

_____, "Judicial Backgrounds and Current Cases,"
     Journal of Criminal Law, Criminology and Police
     Science, 1962, 53: 333-9.

_____ and Neef, Marian, "Racial Disparities That
     Supposedly Don't Exist--Some Pitfalls in Analysis
     of Case Records," Notre Dame Lawyer, October 1976,
     52: 87-94.

_____. The Legal Process from a Behaviorist Per-
     spective. Homeward: Dorsey Press, 1969.

Neubauer, David M. Criminal Justice in Middle America.
     Morristown: General Learning Press, 1974, 240,
     242-3, 249.

Newfield, Jack. Cruel and Unusual Punishment. New York:
     Holt, Rinehart and Winston, 1974, 25.

Nie, Norman H. et al. Statistical Package for the
     Social Sciences, Second Edition. New York:
     Academic Press, 1969.

Nutter, Ralph. "The Quality of Justice in Misdemeanor
     Arraignment Courts," Journal of Criminal Law and
     Criminology, 1962, 53: 215-9.

Oaks, Dallin H. and Lehman, Warren. A Criminal Justice
     System and the Indigent--A Study of Chicago and
     Cook County. Chicago: University of Chicago
     Press, 1968.

Oaks, Dallin. "Lawyers for the Poor," in Abraham
     Blumberg. The Scales of Justice. New York: Aldine,
     1970.

O'Donnell, Pierce, Churgin, Michael, and Curtis,
     Dennis E. Toward a Just and Effective Sentencing
     System--Agenda for Legislative Reform. New York:
     Praeger, 1977.

Packer, Herbert L. The Limits of Criminal Sanctions.
     Stanford: Stanford University Press, 1968.

Pugh, George N. and Carver, Hampton. "Due Process in
    Sentencing--From Mapp to Mempa to McGautha,"
    Texas Law Review, 1971, 49: 25-29.

Radzinowicz, Leon and Wolfgang, Marvin. Crime and
    Justice--The Criminal in the Arms of the Law.
    Vol. II. New York: Basic Books, 1911, 14, 390,392

Reasons, Charles E. "Comment on Methodology, Theory,
    and Ideology," American Sociological Review,
    December 1977, 42: 177-81.

Report of the New York City Board of Corrections,
    "Presentence Reports--Utility or Futility?",
    Fordham Law Journal, 1973, 2: 27-56.

Robison, James, Wildin, Leslie, Carter, Robert and
    Wahl, Albert. The San Francisco Project--A Study
    of Federal Probation and Parole. San Francisco:
    National Institute of Mental Health, 1969.

Rossi, Peter H., Waite, Emily, Rose, Christine E., and
    Berk, Richard. "The Seriousness of Crimes--
    Normative Structure and Individual Differences,"
    American Sociological Review, April 1974, 39:
    224-239.

Seidman, Shan and Zeisel, Diamond Hans. "A Study of
    Sentence Disparity and its Reduction," University
    of Chicago Law Review, 1975, 43: 109-49.

Sellin, Thorsten and Wolfgang, Marvin E. The Measure-
    ment of Delinquency. New York: John Wiley and Sons,
    1964.

Shapiro, Barbara A. and Clement, Catherine. "Pre-Sen-
    tence Information in Felony Cases in Massachusetts
    Superior Court," Suffolk University Law Review,
    1975, 10: 49-75.

Silverstein, Lee. Defense of the Poor for Criminal
    Cases in American State Courts--A Field Study.
    Washington: American Bar Foundation, 1965.

Simon, Herbert A. Models of Man. New York: John Wiley
    and Sons, 1957.

Smith, Alexander and Blumberg, Abraham S. "The Problem of Objectivity on Judicial Decision-Making," Social Forces, September 1967, 46: 96-105.

Somit, Albert, Tannenbaum, Joseph, and Wilks, Walter "Aspects of Judicial Sentence Behavior," University of Pittsburgh Law Review, 1959-1960, 52: 548-55.

Sonquist, John A. Multivariate Model Building. Ann Arbor: University of Michigan Press, 1970.

Sutts, Daniel B., "Uses of Dummy Variables in Regression Equations," American Statistical Association Journal, 1957, 53: 548-55.

Swigert, Victoria and Farrell, Ronald A. Murder, Inequality and the Law--Differential Treatment in the Legal Process. Lexington: Lexington Books, 1976.

_____, "Normal Homicides and the Law," American Sociological Review, February 1977, 42: 16-32.

"Task Force Report--The Courts," In Rodzinowicz, Leon and Wolfgang, Marvin. Crime and Justice. Volume 2. New York: Basic Books, 1971.

Tatsuoka, Maurice and Tredman, David. Discriminant Analysis--The Study of Group Differences. Champaign: Institute of Personality and Ability Testing, 1970.

_____. Multivariate Analysis--Techniques for Educational and Psychological Research. New York: John Wiley and Sons, 1971, 157-93.

Tiffany, Lawrence P., Yakov, Avichai, and Peters, Geoffrey M. "A Statistical Analysis of Sentencing in Federal Courts--Defendants Convicted After Trial," Journal of Legal Studies, 1975, 41: 369-90.

Ungs, Thomas D. and Bass, Gary R. "Judicial Role Perception, A Technique Study of Ohio Judges," Law and Society Review, 1972, 6: 342-66.

Von Hirsch, Andrew. Doing Justice: The Choice of
    Punishment--Report of the Committee for the Study
    of Incarceration. New York: Hill and Wang, 1976.

Walker, Nigel. Sentencing in a Rational Society. New
    York: Basic Books, Inc., 1971.

Weber, Max. Theory of Social and Economic Organi-
    zation. Translated by M. Henderson and Talcott
    Parsons. New York: Free Press, 1947, 424.

Wolfgang, Marvin and Riedel, Marc. "Race, Judicial
    Discretion and the Death Penalty," Annals, 1972,
    407: 119-33.

_____. "Rape, Race, and the Death Penalty,"
    American Journal of Orthopsychiatry, 1975,
    43: 658-68.

Zeisel, Hans. "Methodological Problems in Studies of
    Sentencing," Law and Society Review, May 1967,
    3: 621-31.

APPENDIX

185

Appendix A--Zero Order Correlations--Sample 1[1]

Var.	Corr.[2]	Var.	Corr.	Var.	Corr.	Var.	Corr.
SOC,SFC	.77[3]	SOC,X18	.00	SFC,X3	-.00	SFC,X27	.03
SOC,NA	<u>.04</u>	SOC,X19	-.31	SFC,X4	.05	SFC,X28	.11
SOC,NC	.02	SOC,X20	-.03	SFC,X5	-.00	SFC,X29	.05
SOC,SPA	-.05	SOC,X21	.01	SFC,X6	.05	SFC,X30	.05
SOC,DPC	-.12	SOC,X22	.18	SFC,X7	-.02	SFC,X31	.02
SOC,RPO	.01	SOC,X23	.11	SFC,X8	.00	SFC,X32	.02
SOC,DJ	.04	SOC,X24	-.03	SFC,X9	.01	SFC,X33	.00
SOC,X1	.05	SOC,X25	-.03	SFC,X10	-.05	JA,NC	<u>.81</u>
SOC,X2	-.05	SOC,X26	.01	SFC,X11	.00	NA,SPA	<u>.44</u>
SOC,X3	-.04	SOC,X27	.01	SFC,X12	.04	NA,DPC	-.13
SOC,X4	.03	SOC,X28	.08	SFC,X13	.01	NA,RPO	-.35
SOC,X5	-.02	SOC,X29	.06	SFC,X14	-.21	NA,DJ	-.37
SOC,X6	-.00	SOC,X30	.06	SFC,X15	-.16	NA,X1	-.03
SOC,X7	-.00	SOC,X31	-.05	SFC,X16	-.02	NA,X2	.07
SOC,X8	-.00	SOC,X32	.02	SFC,X17	-.02	NA,X3	-.25
SOC,X9	.04	SOC,X33	.01	SFC,X18	-.02	NA,X4	.12
SOC,X10	-.06	SOC,NA	.02	SFC,X19	-.28	NA,X5	.08
SOC,X11	.00	SOC,NC	.00	SFC,X20	-.01	NA,X6	.08
SOC,X12	.05	SFC,SPA	.02	SFC,X21	.00	NA,X7	.13
SOC,X13	.00	SFC,DPC	-.14	SFC,X22	.18	NA,X8	.05
SOC,X14	-.26	SFC,RPO	.04	SFC,X23	.15	NA,X9	.25
SOC,X15	-.13	SFC,DJ	.05	SFC,X24	-.02	NA,X10	-.07
SOC,X16	.00	SFC,X1	.01	SFC,X25	.01	NA,X11	.23
SOC,X17	-.01	SFC,X2	-.03	SFC,X26	.00	NA,X12	.08
NA,X13	.02	NC,DJ	-.30	NC,X24	.23	SPA,X12	-.16
NA,X14	.00	NC,X1	.02	NC,X25	-.00	SPA,X13	-.03
NA,X15	.03	NC,X2	.05	NC,X26	.10	SPA,X14	-.00
NA,X16	.01	NC,X3	-.24	NC,X27	-.01	SPA,X15	.04
NA,X17	.03	NC,X4	.10	NC,X28	.40	SPA,X16	.04
NA,X18	.04	NC,X5	.07	NC,X29	.31	SPA,X17	-.00
NA,X19	-.02	NC,X6	-.09	NC,X30	-.04	SPA,X18	-.06

[1] See Table 1 for a complete list of variables.

[2] All correlations are rounded to two places.

[3] All correlations of $\pm.50$ or above are underlined.

Var.	Corr.	Var.	Corr.	Var.	Corr.	Var.	Corr.
NA,X20	.37	NC,X7	.12	NC,X31	.00	SPA,X19	.03
NA,X21	.12	NC,X8	.06	NC,X32	.42	SPA,X20	-.26
NA,X22	.81	NC,X9	.18	NC,X33	.54	SPA,X21	-.07
NA,X23	.78	NC,X10	-.01	SPA,DPC	.16	SPA,X22	-.41
NA,X24	.25	NC,X11	.20	SPA,RPO	.29	SPA,X23	-.30
NA,X25	.00	NC,X12	.10	SPA,DJ	.28	SPA,X24	-.14
NA,X26	.13	NC,X13	-.00	SPA,X1	.05	SPA,X25	.05
NA,X27	.03	NC,X14	.04	SPA,X2	-.06	SPA,X26	-.12
NA,X28	.49	NC,X15	-.05	SPA,X3	.15	SPA,X29	-.06
NA,X29	.33	NC,X16	.02	SPA,X4	-.18	SPA,X28	-.14
NA,X30	-.06	NC,X17	.07	SPA,X5	-.02	SPA,X29	-.20
NA,X31	.00	NC,X18	-.01	spa,x6	.07	SPA,X30	.04
NA,X32	.36	NC,X19	-.02	SPA,X7	-.09	SPA,X31	.00
NA,X33	.73	NC,X20	.29	SPA,X8	-.06	SPA,X32	-.14
NC,SPA	-.34	NC,X21	.10	SPA,X9	-.19	SPA,X33	-.31
NC,DPC	-.10	NC,X22	.69	SPA,X10	.03	DPC,RPO	.05
NC,RPO	-.28	NC,X23	.96	SPA,X11	-.19	DPC,DJ	.06
DPC,X1	-.02	DPC,X25	-.02	RPO,X15	.01	DJ,X6	.20
DPC,X2	.02	DPC,X26	-.04	RPO,X16	.04	DJ,X7	-.06
DPC,X3	.04	DPC,X27	.03	RPO,X17	-.03	DJ,X8	.01
DPC,X4	-.02	DPC,X28	-.05	RPO,X18	-.10	DJ,X9	-.18
DPC,X5	-.03	DPC,X29	-.06	RPO,X19	.00	DJ,X10	.12
DPC,X6	-.02	DPC,X30	-.01	RPO,X20	-.42	DJ,X11	-.29
DPC,X7	-.04	DPC,X31	-.01	RPO,X21	-.16	DJ,X12	.06
DPC,X8	-.06	DPC,x32	-.05	RPO,X22	-.02	DJ,X13	-.08
DPC,X9	-.07	DPC,X33	-0.09	RPO,X23	-.26	DJ,X14	.00
DPC,X10	.04	RPO,DJ	.74	rpo,x24	-.23	DJ,X15	-.01
DPC,X11	-.06	RPO,X1	.07	RPO,X25	.15	DJ,X16	.04
DPC,X12	-.05	RPO,X2	-.06	RPO,X26	-.17	DJ,X17	-.01
DPC,X13	.02	RPO,X3	-.07	RPO,X27	-.10	DJ,X18	-.10
DPC,X14	-.01	RPO,X4	-.13	RPO,X28	-.22	DJ,X19	.00
DPC,X15	-.00	RPO,X5	.06	RPO,X29	.02	DJ,X20	-.47
DPC,X16	-.02	RPO,X6	.20	RPO,X30	.18	DJ,X21	-.19
DPC,X17	-.01	RPO,X7	-.10	RPO,X31	.04	DJ,X22	-.12
DPC,X18	.03	RPO,X8	.03	RPO,X32	-.07	DJ,X23	-.27
DPC,X19	-.00	RPO,X9	-.19	RPO,X33	-.27	DJ,X24	-.22
DPC,X20	-.08	RPO,X10	.12	DJ,X1	.07	DJ,X25	.14
DPC,X21	.00	RPO,X11	-.30	DJ,X2	-.07	DJ,X26	-.14
DPC,X22	-.12	RPO,X12	.07	DJ,X3	-.04	DJ,X27	-.10

Var.	Corr.	Var.	Corr.	Var.	Corr.	Var.	Corr.
DPC,X23	-.11	RPO,X13	-.06	DJ,X4	-.08	DJ,X28	-.21
DPC,X24	-.04	RPO,X14	-.02	DJ,X5	.07	DJ,X29	-.00
DJ,X30	.14	X1,X22	.02	X2,X15	-.13	X3,X9	-.15
DJ,X31	.06	X1,X23	.02	X2,X16	-.44	X3,X10	-.26
DJ,X32	-.09	X1,X24	-.07	X2,X17	-.11	X3,X11	.00
DJ,X33	-.28	X1,X25	.00	X2,X18	.25	X3,X12	-.06
X1,X2	-.53	X1,X26	-.05	X2,X19	.15	X3,X13	.08
X1,X3	-.02	X1,X27	-.41	X2,X20	.08	X3,X14	-.00
X1,X4	-.10	X1,X28	-.02	X2,X21	.17	X3,X15	.05
X1,X5	-.03	X1,X29	.02	X2,X22	.02	X3,X16	-.00
X1,X6	.03	X1,X30	.67	X2,X23	.03	X3,X17	-.04
X1,X7	-.03	X1,X31	-.28	X2,X24	.05	X3,X18	.08
X1,X8	.01	X1,X32	.53	X2,X25	-.12	X3,X19	.04
X1,X9	-.08	X1,X33	-.25	X2,X26	.04	X3,X20	-.03
X1,X10	.05	X2,X3	.03	X2,X27	.25	X3,X21	.06
X1,X11	-.07	X2,X4	-.10	X2,X28	.06	X3,X22	-.24
X1,X12	.01	X2,X5	-.13	X2,X29	.05	X3,X23	-.22
X1,X13	.19	X2,X6	-.06	X2,X30	-.36	X3,X24	-.07
X1,X14	-.18	X2,X7	.02	X2,X31	.53	X3,X25	-.21
X1,X15	-.08	X2,X8	.01	X2,X32	-.29	X3,X26	-.10
X1,X16	.82	X2,X9	.06	X2,X33	.46	X3,X27	-.08
X1,X17	.21	X2,X10	-.02	X3,X4	.07	X3,X29	-.13
X1,X18	-.41	X2,X11	.11	X3,X5	-.28	X3,X30	-.01
X1,X19	-.26	X2,X12	-.04	X3,X6	.05	X3,X31	.06
X1,X20	-.08	X2,X13	-.08	X3,X7	-.17	X3,X32	-.09
X1,X21	-.15	X2,X14	.25	X3,X8	-.29	X3,X33	-.16
X4,X5	.03	X4,X29	.02	X5,X25	.70	X6X22	-.04
X4,X6	.20	X4,X30	.03	X5,X26	-.03	X6,X23	-.08
Y4,X7	.05	X4,X31	.12	X5,X27	-.05	X6,X24	-.08
X4,X8	-.10	C3,X32	.06	X5,X28	.04	X6,X25	.45
X4,X9	-.00	X4,X33	.04	X5,X29	.02	X6, X26	-.08
X4,X10	-.06	X5,X6	.11	X5,X30	.03	X6,X27	.10
X4,X11	.09	X5,X7	-.01	X5,X31	-.02	X6,X28	-.06
X4,X12	.01	X5,X8	.14	X5,X32	-.02	X6,X29	-.04
X4,X13	.07	X5,X9	-.04	X5,X33	.02	X6,X30	.35
X4,X14	.00	X5,X10	.15	X6,X7	-.05	X6,X31	.58
X4,X15	.05	X5,X11	.06	X6,X8	-.01	X6,X32	-.04
X4,X16	-.01	X5,X12	.01	X6,X9	-.15	X6,X33	-.05

Var.	Corr.	Var.	Corr.	Var.	Corr.	Var.	Corr.
X4,X17	.00	X5,X13	-.07	X6,X10	.08	X7,X8	-.54
X4,X18	-.06	X5,X14	.00	X6,X11	-.12	X7,X9	.11
X4,X19	.04	X5,X15	.06	X6,X12	-.01	X7,X10	.12
X4,X20	.10	X5,X16	-.04	X6,X13	-.09	X7,X11	.06
X4,X21	-.03	X5,X17	.02	X6,X14	.06	X7,X12	-.06
X4,X22	.11	X5,X18	-.05	X6,X15	.07	X7,X13	-.00
X4,X23	.09	X5,X19	.04	X6,X16	.02	X7,X14	.04
X4,X24	.05	X5,X20	-.03	X6,X17	-.00	X7,X15	.00
X4,X25	.07	X5,X21	-.11	X6,X18	-.10	X7,X16	-.00
X4,X26	.03	X5,X22	.07	X6,X19	.09	X7,X17	-.03
X4,X27	-.07	X5,X23	.07	X6,X20	-.15	X7,X18	-.00
X4,X28	.06	X5,X24	-.05	X6,X21	-.20	X7,X19	.04
X7,X20	.10	X8,X19	.02	X9,X19	.01	X10,X20	-.11
X7,X21	.06	X8,X20	.01	X9,X20	.25	X10,X21	.08
X7,X22	.09	X8,X21	-.02	X9,X21	.10	X10,X22	-.06
X7,X23	.11	X8,X22	.06	X9,X22	.20	X10,X23	-.04
X7,X24	.57	X8,X23	.06	X9,X23	.18	X10,X24	-.03
X7,X25	.01	X8,X24	-.31	X9,X24	.16	X10,X25	.17
X7,X26	.62	X8,X25	.10	X9,X25	-.08	X10,X26	-.26
X7,X27	-.00	X8,X26	-.33	X9,X26	.42	X10,X27	-.08
X7,X28	.04	X8,X27	-.05	X9,X27	.03	X10,X28	-.10
X7,X29	-.00	X8,X28	.05	X9,X28	.20	X10,X29	-.04
X7,X30	-.02	X8,X29	.08	X9,X29	.13	X10,X30	.05
X7,X31	.00	X8,X30	-.01	X9,X30	-.09	X10,X31	.03
X7,X32	.04	X8,X31	-.02	X9,X31	-.05	X10,X32	-.00
X7,X33	.10	X8,X32	.03	X9,X32	.06	X10,X33	-.05
X8,X9	.18	X8,X33	.02	X9,X33	.17	X11,X12	-.21
X8,X10	.35	X9,X10	-.62	X10,X11	-.11	X11,X13	-.03
X8,X11	.07	X9,X11	.27	X10,X12	-.04	X11,X14	-.03
X8,X12	.08	X9,X12	.07	X10,X13	-.07	X11,X15	.01
X8,X13	-.06	X9,X13	.01	X10,X14	.06	X11,X16	-.03
X8,X14	.04	X9,X14	.00	X10,X15	.03	X11,X17	-.02
X8,X15	-.00	X9,X15	-.02	X10,X16	.00	X11,X18	.05
X8,X16	-.00	X9,X16	-.03	X10,X17	.08	X11,X19	-.02
X8,X17	.04	X9,X17	-.07	X10,X18	-.08	X11,X10	.31
X8,X18	-.05	X9,X18	.04	X10,X19	.04	X11,X21	.10

Var.	Corr.	Var.	Corr.	Var.	Corr.	Var.	Corr.
X11,X22	.13	X12,X25	-.03	X13,X29	-.00	X15,X16	-.11
X11,X23	.19	X12,X26	-.04	X13,X30	.11	X15,X17	.2-
X11,X24	.14	X12,X27	.02	X13,X31	-.11	X15,X18	-.22
X11,X25	-.09	X12,X28	-.13	X13,X32	.11	X15,X19	.46
X11,X26	.11	X12,X29	.69	X13,X33	-.01	X15,X20	-.02
X11,X27	.05	X12,X30	.01	X14,X15	-.11	X15,X21	-.00
X11,X28	.63	X12,X31	-.03	X14,X16	-.18	X15,X22	-.04
X11,X29	-.15	X12,X32	.06	X14,X17	.09	X15,X23	-.05
X11,X30	-.09	X12,X33	-.00	X14,X18	-.34	X15,X24	.02
X11,X31	-.00	X13,X14	-.47	X14,X19	.77	X15,X25	.07
X11,X32	.07	X13,X15	-.30	X14,X20	.01	X15,X26	-.02
X11,X33	.20	X13,X16	.37	X14,X21	.02	X15,X27	-.22
X12,X13	.03	X13,X17	-.12	X14,X22	-.05	X15,X28	-.02
X12,X14	-.05	X13,X18	.73	X14,X23	.00	X15,X29	-.03
X12,X15	.00	X13,X19	-.57	X14,X24	-.00	X15,X30	-.07
X12,X16	.00	X13,X20	.06	X14,X25	.05	X15,X31	-.03
X12,X17	.02	X13,X21	.02	X14,X26	.04	X15,X32	-.03
X12,X18	.02	X13,X22	.00	X14,X27	-.35	X15,X33	-.07
X12,X19	-.05	X13,X23	-.01	X14,X28	-.04	X17,X18	-.09
X12,X20	-.08	X13,X24	.00	X14,X29	-.05	X17,X19	-.06
X12,X21	.05	X13,X25	-.11	X14,X30	-.12	X17,X20	.04
X12,X22	.19	X13,X26	-.03	X14,X31	.19	X17,X21	-.02
X12,X23	.09	X13,X27	.73	X14,X32	-.09	X17,X22	.02
X12,X24	-.05	X13,X28	.00	X14,X33	.09	X17,X23	.08
X17,X24	-.03	X18,X33	.14	X20,X30	-.13	X22,X31	-.01
X17,X25	.00	X19,X20	-.02	X20,X31	-.02	X22,X32	.43
X17,X26	-.03	X19,X21	.01	X20,X32	.08	X22,X33	.51
X17,X27	-.08	X19,X22	-.08	X20,X33	.30	X23,X24	.20
X17,X28	-.02	X19,X23	-.06	X21,X22	.07	X23,X25	-.00
X17,X29	-.00	X19,X24	.02	X21,X23	.08	X23,X26	.09
X17,X30	.12	X19,X25	.08	X21,X24	.10	X23,X27	-.02
X17,X31	-.06	X19,X26	.04	X21,X25	-.17	X23,X28	.47
X17,X32	.17	X19,X27	-.43	X21,X26	.06	X23,X29	.31
X17,X33	-.05	X19,X28	-.05	X21,X27	.11	X23,X30	-.03
X18,X19	-.43	X19,X29	-.07	X21,X28	.08	X23,X31	-.00
X18,X20	.10	X19,X30	-.18	X21,X29	.04	X23,X32	.40
X18,X21	.11	X19,X31	.15	X21,X30	-.20	X23,X33	.52
X18,X22	-.00	X19,X32	-.14	X21,X31	.02	X24,X25	-.03

Appendix A--Zero Order Correlations--Sample 1 (Cnt'd)

Var.	Corr.	Var.	Corr.	Var.	Corr.	Var.	Corr.
X18,X23	-.02	X19,X33	.04	X21,X32	-.06	X24,X26	.53
X18,X24	.04	X20,X21	.21	X21,X33	.14	X24,X27	.04
X18,X25	-.09	X20,X22	.19	X22,X23	.72	X24,X28	.11
X18,X26	-.01	X20,X23	.26	X22,X24	.13	X24,X29	.00
X18,X27	1.00	X20,X24	.44	X22,X25	.01	X24,X30	-.07
X18,X28	.00	X20,X25	-.06	X22,X26	.07	X24,X31	-.00
X18,X29	-.00	X20,X26	.17	X22,X27	-.00	X24,X32	.05
X18,X30	-.28	X20,X27	.10	X22,X28	.40	X24,X33	.21
X18,X31	.07	X20,X28	.26	X22,X29	.48	X25,X26	-.03
X18,X32	-.22	X20,X29	-.00	X22,X30	.00	X25,X27	-.10
X25,X28	-.00	X26,X29	-.00	X27,X31	.06	X29,X31	-.06
X25,X29	-.02	X26,X30	-.06	X27,X32	-.22	X29,X32	.23
X24,X30	.15	X26,X31	-.02	X27,X33	.14	X29,X33	.09
X25,X31	.16	X26,X32	-.00	X28,X29	-.09	X30,X31	-.19
X25,X32	.02	X26,X33	.10	X28,X30	-.06	X30,X32	.27
X25,X33	-.03	X27,X28	.00	X28,X31	.00	X30,X33	- .7
X26,X27	-.01	X27,X29	.00	X28,X32	.18	X31,X32	-.15
X26,X28	.00	X27,X30	-.28	X28,X33	.38	X31,X33	.21
				X29,X30	.03	X32,X33	21

Var.	Corr.
X16,X17	-.04
X16,X18	-.34
X16,X19	-.22
X16,X20	-.06
X16,X21	-.12
X16,X22	.01
X16,X23	.01
X16,X24	-.05
X16,X25	-.01
X16,X26	-.03
X16,X27	.01
X16,X28	.01
X16,X29	.54
X16,X30	.54
X16,X31	.23
X16,X32	.49
X16,X33	-.20

191

Appendix B--Zero Order Correlations--Sample 2[1]

Var.	Corr.[2]	Var.	Corr.	Var.	Corr.	Var.	Corr.
SOC,SFC	.54[3]	SOC,Y19	-.03	SFC,Y13	-.10	NA,Y8	-.05
SOC,NA	-.13	SOC,Y20	-.03	SFC,Y14	-.06	NA,Y9	.14
SOC,NC	-.06	SOC,Y21	-.13	SFC,Y15	.00	YA,Y10	.02
SOC,SPA	.30	SOC,Y22	.12	SFC,Y16	-.20	NA,Y11	.05
SOC,DPC	.13	SOC,Y23	-.05	SFC,Y17	-.21	NA,Y12	.04
SOC,DJ	.24	SOC,Y24	-.03	SFC,Y18	-.05	NA,Y13	.00
SOC,Y1	.01	SOC,Y25	-.00	SFC,Y19	.01	NA,Y14	.03
SOC,Y2	-.06	SFC,NA	-.20	SFC,Y20	.00	NA,Y15	.00
SOC,Y3	-.05	SFC,NC	-.12	SFC,Y21	-.23	NA,Y16	.05
SOC,Y4	-.07	SFC,SPA	.31	SFC,Y22	.26	NA,Y17	.04
SOC,Y5	-.05	SFC,DPC	.18	SFC,Y23	-.05	NA,Y18	.09
SOC,Y6	-.07	SFC,DJ	.36	SFC,Y24	-.07	NA,Y19	-.06
SOC,Y7	-.14	SFC,Y1	.08	SFC,Y25	.00	NA,Y20	-.07
SOC,Y8	-.13	SFC,Y2	-.08	NA,NC	.83	NA,Y21	.21
SOC,Y9	-.10	SFC,Y3	-.05	NA,SPA	.52	NA,Y22	.36
SOC,Y10	.04	sfc,y4	.03	NA,DPC	-.67	NA,Y23	.97
SOC,Y11	-.30	SFC,Y5	-.06	NA,DJ	.36	NA,Y24	.18
SOC,Y12	-.32	SFC,Y6	-.03	NA,Y1	-.03	NA,Y25	.40
SOC,Y13	-.24	SFC,Y7	-.08	NA,Y2	.13	NC,SPA	-.32
SOC,Y14	-.17	SFC,Y8	-.07	NA,Y3	-.04	NC,DPC	-.61
SOC,Y15	-.12	SFC,Y9	-.16	NA,Y4	-.10	NC,DJ	-.25
SOC,Y16	-.22	SFC,Y10	.02	NA,Y5	.07	NC,Y1	-.03
SOC,Y17	-.39	SFC,Y11	-.20	NA,Y6	-.02	NC,Y2	.11
SOC,Y18	-.03	SFC,Y12	-.18	NA,Y7	-.00	NC,Y3	-.04
NC,Y4	-.10	SPA,Y1	.07	SPA,Y25	-.25	DPC,Y23	-.63
NC,Y5	.08	SPA,Y2	-.18	DPC,DJ	.31	DPC,Y24	-.17
NC,Y6	.00	SPA,Y3	-.00	DPC,Y1	-.00	DPC,Y25	-.29
NC,Y7	-.02	SPA,Y4	.01	DPC,Y2	-.09	DJ,Y1	.09

[1]See Table 1 for a complete list of variables.

[2]All correlations are rounded to two places.

[3]All correlations of ±.50 or more are underlined.

Var.	Corr.	Var.	Corr.	Var.	Corr.	Var.	Corr.
NC,Y8	-.04	SPA,Y5	-.09	DPC,Y3	.03	DJ,Y2	.16
NC,Y9	.12	SPA,Y6	-.02	DPC,Y4	.12	DJ,Y3	.04
NC,Y10	-.01	SPA,Y7	-.12	DPC,Y5	-.10	DJ,Y4	.01
NC,Y11	.00	SPA,Y8	-.09	DPC,Y6	-.02	DJ,Y5	.04
NC,Y12	.05	SPA,Y9	-.12	DPC,Y7	-.04	DJ,Y6	.02
NC,Y13	-.02	SPA,Y10	-.09	DPC,Y8	.02	DJ,Y7	-.09
NC,Y14	.02	SPA,Y11	-.12	dpc,y9	-.13	DJ,Y8	.04
NC,Y15	.03	SPA,Y12	-.19	DPC,Y10	-.02	DJ,Y9	-.19
NC,Y16	.00	SPA,Y13	-.06	DPC,Y11	-.07	DJ,Y10	-.00
NC,Y17	.03	SPA,Y14	-.02	DPC,Y12	-.10	DJ,Y11	-.16
NC,Y18	.08	SPA,Y15	-.01	DPC,Y13	-.00	DJ,Y12	-.16
NC,Y19	-.04	SPA,Y16	-.14	DPC,Y14	-.06	DJ,Y13	-.06
NC,Y20	-.04	SPA,Y17	-.20	DPC,Y15	-.00	DJ,Y14	-.04
NC,Y21	.14	SPA,Y18	-.11	DPC,Y16	-.05	DJ,Y15	-.02
NC,Y22	-.28	SPA,Y19	-.00	DPC,Y17	-.09	DJ,Y16	-.16
NC,Y23	.78	SPA,Y20	-.07	DPC,Y18	-.08	DJ,Y17	-.17
NC,Y24	.14	SPA,Y21	-.15	DPC,Y19	.01	DJ,Y18	-.15
NC,Y25	.31	SPA,Y22	-.22	DPC,Y20	.06	DJ,Y19	.09
SPA,DPC	.50	SPA,Y23	-.49	DPC,Y21	-.21	DJ,Y20	.06
SPA,DJ	.31	SPA,Y24	-.12	DPC,Y22	.32	DJ,Y21	-.44
DJ,Y22	.72	Y1,Y21	-.04	Y2,Y21	.08	Y3,Y22	.08
DJ,Y23	.29	Y1,Y22	.06	Y2,Y22	-.15	Y3,Y23	-.06
DJ,Y24	-.14	Y1,Y23	-.04	Y2,Y23	.15	Y3,Y24	-.01
DJ,Y25	-.08	Y1,Y24	-.03	Y2,Y24	.05	Y3,Y25	-.02
Y1,Y2	-.53	Y1,Y25	-.02	Y2,Y25	.07	Y4,Y5	.03
Y1,Y3	-.28	Y2,Y3	-.52	Y3,Y4	-.03	Y4,Y6	-.18
Y1,Y4	.06	Y2,Y4	-.05	Y3,Y5	.12	Y4,Y7	.42
Y1,Y5	.05	Y2,Y5	-.17	Y3,Y6	.19	Y4,Y8	.10
Y1,Y6	-.06	Y2,Y6	-.07	Y3,Y7	.04	Y4,Y9	-.05
Y1,Y7	-.06	Y2,Y7	.06	Y3,Y8	.08	Y4,Y10	.04
Y1,Y8	-.03	Y2,Y8	.00	Y3,Y9	.03	Y4,Y11	.07
Y1,Y9	-.03	Y2,Y9	.08	Y3,Y10	.02	y4,Y12	-.00
Y1,Y10	-.07	Y2,Y10	.06	Y3,Y11	-.00	Y4,Y13	-.01

Var.	Corr.	Var.	Corr.	Var.	Corr.	Var.	Corr.
Y1,Y11	.16	Y2,Y11	-.07	Y3,Y12	-.08	Y4,Y14	.06
Y1,Y12	-.14	Y2,Y12	.22	Y3,Y13	.33	Y4,Y15	.06
Y1,Y13	-.09	Y2,Y13	-.17	Y3,Y14	-.19	Y4,Y16	.02
Y1,Y14	.59	Y2,Y14	-.31	Y3,Y15	-.04	Y4,Y17	-.03
Y1,Y15	.13	Y2,Y15	-.06	Y3,Y16	.13	Y4,Y18	.09
Y1,Y16	-.25	Y2,Y16	.17	Y3,Y17	.15	Y4,Y19	-.00
Y1,Y17	-.21	Y2,Y17	.10	Y3,Y18	-.03	Y4,Y20	-.11
Y1,Y18	-.07	Y2,Y18	.07	Y3,Y19	.04	Y4,Y21	-.04
Y1,Y19	.08	Y2,Y19	-.08	Y3,Y20	-.00	Y4,Y22	.08
Y1,Y20	.04	Y2,Y20	.02	Y3,Y21	-.02	Y4,Y23	-.11
Y4,Y24	-.04	Y6,Y9	.10	Y7,Y15	.06	Y8,Y22	.06
Y4,Y25	-.07	Y6,Y10	-.07	Y7,Y16	.08	Y8,Y23	-.04
Y5,Y6	.07	Y6,Y11	-.07	Yu,Y17	.06	Y8,Y24	.02
Y5,Y7	-.02	Y6,Y12	.05	Y7,Y18	.11	Y8,Y25	-.03
Y5,Y8	.16	Y6,Y13	.16	Y7,Y19	-.02	Y9,Y10	-.01
Y5,Y9	-.23	Y6,Y14	.00	Y7,Y20	-.08	Y9,Y11	.10
Y5,Y10	.01	Y6,Y15	.02	Y7,Y21	.02	Y9,Y12	-.04
Y5,Y11	-.04	Y6,Y16	-.07	Y7,Y22	-.01	Y9,Y13	.04
Y5,Y12	.01	Y6,Y17	.13	Y7,Y23	-.02	Y9,Y14	.04
Y5,Y13	.06	Y6,Y18	-.09	Y7,Y24	.00	Y9,Y15	.02
Y5,Y14	-.00	Y6,Y19	.05	Y7,Y25	-.00	Y9,Y16	.09
Y5,Y15	.04	Y6,Y20	.11	Y8,Y9	-.37	Y9,Y17	-.02
Y5,Y16	-.05	Y6,Y21	.01	Y8,Y10	-.10	Y9,Y18	.09
Y5,Y17	.04	Y6,Y22	-.01	Y8,Y11	-.05	Y9,Y19	-.05
Y5,Y18	.01	Y6,Y23	-.03	Y8,Y12	.07	Y9,Y20	-.01
Y5,Y19	.03	Y6,Y24	-.04	Y8,Y13	.06	Y9,Y21	.05
Y5,Y20	-.02	Y6,Y25	-.06	Y8,Y14	-.02	Y9,Y22	-.16
Y5,Y21	.04	Y7,Y8	.23	Y8.Y15	.00	Y9,Y23	.10
Y5,Y22	-.00	Y7,Y9	.17	Y8,Y16	-.04	Y9,Y24	-.02
Y5,Y23	.05	Y7,Y10	.01	Y8,Y17	.10	Y9,Y25	-.00
Y5,Y24	.05	Y7,Y11	.07	Y8,Y18	-.09	Y10,Y11	.01
Y5,Y25	.05	Y7,Y12	.08	Y8,Y19	.05	Y10,Y12	.00
Y6,Y7	-.18	Y7,Y13	.00	Y8,Y20	.13	Y10,Y13	-.00
Y6,Y8	.26	Y7,Y14	.00	Y8,Y21	.00	Y10,Y14	.03

Var.	Corr.	Var.	Corr.	Var.	Corr.	Var.	Corr.
Y10,Y15	-.05	Y11,Y25	.01	Y13,Y24	.05	Y16,Y18	.05
Y10,Y16	.00	Y12,Y13	-.07	Y13,Y25	-.00	Y16,Y19	-.03
Y10,Y17	.00	Y12,Y14	-.11	Y14,Y15	-.03	Y16,Y20	.00
Y10,Y18	.06	Y12,Y15	.16	Y14,Y16	-.15	Y16,Y21	.12
Y10,Y19	-.04	Y12,Y16	-.16	Y14,Y17	-.13	Y16,Y22	-.11
Y10,Y20	-.07	Y12,Y17	.77	Y14,Y18	-.01	Y16,Y23	.01
Y10,Y21	.05	Y12,Y18	.00	Y14,Y19	.05	Y16,Y24	.11
Y10,Y22	-.01	Y12,Y19	.03	Y14,Y20	-.03	Y16,Y25	.00
Y10,Y23	.03	Y12,Y20	.02	Y14,Y21	.04	Y17,Y18	.04
Y10,Y24	.22	Y12,Y21	.11	Y14,Y22	-.05	Y17,Y19	.00
Y10,Y25	.48	Y12,Y22	-.11	Y14,Y23	.00	Y17,Y20	-.00
Y11,Y12	-.21	Y12,Y23	.03	Y14,Y24	.01	Y17,Y21	.13
Y11,Y13	-.14	Y12,Y24	-.02	Y14,Y25	.01	Y17,Y22	-.10
Y11,Y14	.50	Y12,Y25	-.00	Y15,Y16	-.04	Y17,Y23	.02
Y11,Y15	-.05	Y13,Y14	-.05	Y15,Y17	-.03	Y1y,Y24	.02
Y11,Y16	.76	Y13,Y15	.12	Y15,Y18	-.02	Y17,Y25	-.00
Y11,Y17	-.25	Y13,Y16	-.11	Y15,Y19	-.02	Y18,Y19	-.50
Y11,Y18	.04	Y13,Y17	.51	Y15,Y20	.06	Y18,Y20	-.65
Y11,Y19	.01	Y13,Y18	.05	Y15,Y21	-.02	Y18,Y21	.10
Y11,Y20	-.02	Y13,Y19	-.13	Y15,Y22	-.00	Y18,Y22	-.15
Y11,Y21	.13	Y13,Y20	.00	Y14,Y23	.00	Y18,Y23	.08
Y11,Y22	-.12	Y13,Y21	.04	Y15,Y24	-.01	Y18,Y24	.03
Y11,Y23	.00	Y13,Y22	-.03	Y15,Y25	-.02	Y18,Y25	.03
Y11,Y24	.10	Y13,Y23	-.01	Y16,Y17	-.19	Y19,Y20	-.09
Y19,Y21	-.06	Y20,Y21	-.06	Y21,Y22	-.66	Y22,Y24	-.29
Y19,Y22	.08	Y20,Y22	.10	Y21,Y23	.15	Y22,Y25	-.13
Y19,Y23	-.06	Y20,Y23	-.05	Y21,Y24	.43	Y23,Y24	.16
Y19,Y24	-.03	Y20,Y24	.01	Y21,Y25	.12	Y23,Y25	.44
Y19,Y25	-.03	Y20,Y25	-.01	Y22,Y23	-.30	Y24,Y25	.39

Appendix C--Zero Order Correlations[1]--Sample 3

Var.	Corr.[2]	Var.	Corr.	Var.	Corr.	Var.	Corr.
SOC,SFC	.47	SFC,Z9	.05	SPA,Z11	.05	Z3,Z7	.08
SOC,NA	.27	SFC,Z11	.13	SPA,Z12	.00	Z3,Z8	-.06
SOC,SPA	-.13	SFC,Z12	-.21	DJ,Z2	-.15	Z3,Z9	.13
SOC,DJ	-.02	NA,SPA	-.21	DJ,Z3	-.04	Z3,Z11	.08
SOC,Z2[4]	-.26	NA,DJ	-.29	DJ,Z4	-.20	Z3,Z12	.02
SOC,Z3	-.17	NA,Z2	.07	DJ,Z5	-.11	Z4,Z5	.00
SOC,Z4	.09	NA,Z3	-.29	DJ,Z6	-.07	Z4,Z6	-.09
SOC,Z5	.04	NA,Z4	.08	DJ,Z7	.08	Z4,Z7	-.16
SOC,Z6	.04	NA,Z5	.12	DJ,Z8	-.08	Z4,Z8	.05
SOC,Z7	.17	NA,Z6	.26	DJ,Z9	.11	Z4,Z9	.10
SOC,Z8	-.35	NA,Z7	-.10	DJ,Z11	.02	Z4,Z11	-.18
SOC,Z9	-.02	NA,Z8	.12	DJ,Z12	.00	Z4,Z12	.20
SOC,Z11[4]	.15	NA,Z9	-.15	Z2,Z3	.08	Z5,Z6	.11
SOC,Z12	-.32	NA,Z11	-.11	Z2,Z4	-.07	Z5,Z7	.11
SFC,NA	.21	NA,Z12	-.03	Z2,Z5	-.11	Z5,Z8	.06
SFC,SPA	.04	SPA,DJ	.22	Z2,Z6	.02	Z5,Z9	-.15
SFC,DJ	.04	SPA,Z2	.10	Z2,Z7	-.31	Z5,Z11	.04
SFC,Z2	-.09	SPA,Z3	.08	Z2,Z8	.47	Z5,Z12	-.08
SFC,Z3	.03	SPA,Z4	-.16	Z2,Z9	-.19	Z6,Z7	.00
SFC,Z4	.07	SPA,Z5	-.06	Z2,Z11	-.20	Z6,Z8	.11
SFC,Z5	-.06	SPA,Z6	-.06	Z2,Z12	.30	Z6,Z9	-.05
SFC,Z6	-.04	SPA,Z7	.05	Z3,Z4	.03	Z6,Z11	.00
SFC,Z7	.09	SPA,Z8	.03	Z3,Z5	-.11	Z6,Z12	.05
SFC,Z8	-.27	SPA,Z9	.00	Z3,Z6	-.27	Z7,Z8	-.58[3]
Z7,Z9	-.39	Z7,Z12	.83	Z8,Z11	-.53	Z9,Z11	.36
Z7,Z11	.92	Z8,Z9	.28	Z8,Z12	.69	Z9,Z12	.47
						Z11,Z12	-.77

[1]See Table 1 for complete list of variables.

[2]All correlations are rounded to two places.

[3]Correlations of ±.50 or above are underlined.

[4]The variables Z1 and Z10 were eliminated due to the small number of cases for these catagories.

Appendix D--Standard Deviations of the Variables--
Sample 1[1]

Var.	S.D.	Var.	S.D.	Var.	S.D.	Var.	S.D.
SOC	.49[2]	X3	.42	X13	.50	X23	4.8
SFC	.42	X4	.31	X14	.36	X24	.25
NA	4.0	X5	.45	X15	.25	X25	.37
NC	2.4	X6	.50	X16	.36	X26	.27
SPA	1.0	X7	.39	X17	.11	X27	.49
DPC	6.5	X8	.50	X18	.49	X28	5.7
RPO	.92	X9	.47	X19	.41	X29	4.1
DJ	.96	X10	.50	X20	.44	X30	.30
X1	.40	X11	.35	X21	.41	X31	.43
X2	.50	X12	.40	X22	14.3	X32	2.1
						X33	3.6

[1]See Table 1 for a complete list of the variables.

[2]All standard deviations are rounded to two places.

Appendix E--Standard Deviations of the Variables--Sample 2[1]

Var.	S.D.	Var.	S.D.	Var.	S.D.	Var.	S.D.
SOC	.68[2]	Y2	.50	Y10	.43	Y18	.41
SFC	.56	Y3	.41	Y11	.45	Y19	.25
NA	4.3	Y4	.33	Y12	.30	Y20	.31
NC	2.1	Y5	.36	Y13	.21	Y21	.27
SPA	1.1	Y6	.31	Y14	.29	Y22	.37
DPC	1.3	Y7	.40	Y15	.08	Y23	1.0
DJ	1.2	Y8	.46	Y16	.39	Y24	2.5
Y1	.41	Y9	.43	Y17	.34	Y25	6.0

[1]See Table 1 for a complete list of variables.

[2]All standard deviations are rounded to two places.

Appendix F--Standard Deviations of the Variables--Sample 3[1]

Var.	S.D.	Var.	S.D.	Var.	S.D.	Var.	S.D.
SOC	.51[2]	DJ	.80	Z4	.22	Z8	.46
SFC	.33	Z1	.20	Z5	.49	Z9	.37
NA	.44	Z2	.48	Z6	.43	Z10	.19
SPA	.64	Z3	.44	Z7	.50	Z11	.49
						Z12	.50

[1]See Table 1 for complete list of the variables.

[2]All standard deviations are rounded to two places.

Appendix G

Table 1: Variables in the Analysis

Sample 1 Variable	Sample 2 Variable	Sample 3 Variable
$X1^b$=Dummy variable for ethnicity of defendant, coded 1 for White, 0 otherwise.	$Y1^b$=Dummy variable for ethnicity of defendant, coded 1 for White, 0 otherwise.	$Z1^b$=Dummy variable for ethnicity of defendant, coded 1 for White, 0 otherwise.
$X2$= Dummy variable for ethnicity of defendant, coded 1 for Black, 0 otherwise.	$Y2$= Dummy variable for ethnicity of defendant, coded 1 for Black, 0 otherwise.	$Z2$= Dummy variable for ethnicity of defendant, coded 1 for Black, 0 otherwise.
$X3$= Dummy variable for age, coded 1 for age under 19, 0 otherwise.	$Y3$= Dummy variable for ethnicity of defendant, coded 1 for Puerto Rican, 0 otherwise.	$Z3$= Dummy variable for age, coded 1 for age under 19, 0 otherwise.
$X4$= Dummy variable for sex, coded 1 for male, 0 otherwise.	$Y4$= Dummy variable for age, coded 1 for age under 19, 0 otherwise	$Z4$= Dummy variable for sex, coded 1 for male, 0 otherwise.
$X5$= Dummy variable for marital status, coded 1 for married, 0 otherwise.		$Z5$= Dummy variable for promises, coded 1 for promises, 0 otherwise.

aSee Chapter III for scaling of the variables.

bVariables designated X are from sample 1, variables designated Y from sample 2, and variables designated Z from sample 3.

200

Appendix G (cnt'd)

Table 1: Variables in the Analysis[a]

Sample 1 Variable	Sample 2 Variable	Sample 3 Variable
X6[b]=Dummy variable for employment status, coded 1 for employed, 0 otherwise.	Y5[b]=Dummy variable for sex, coded 1 for male, 0 otherwise.	Z6[b]=Dummy variable for warrants, coded 1 for warrants, 0 otherwise.
X7= Dummy variable for promises, coded 1 for promises, 0 otherwise.	Y6= Dummy variable for marital status, coded 1 for married, 0 otherwise.	Z7= Dummy variable for ethnicity of complainant, coded 1 for White, 0 otherwise.
X8= Dummy variable for promises, coded 1 for no promises, 0 otherwise.	Y7= Dummy variable for marital status, coded 1 for unmarried, 0 otherwise.	Z8= Dummy variable for ethnicity of complainant, coded 1 for Black, 0 otherwise.
X9= Dummy variable for warrants, coded 1 for warrants, 0 otherwise.	Y8= Dummy variable for employment status, coded 1 for employed, 0 otherwise.	Z9= Dummy variable for ethnicity of complainant, coded 1 for Puerto Rican, 0 otherwise.

[a]See Chapter III for scaling of the variables.

[b]Variables designed X are from sample 1, variables designated Y from sample 2, and variables designated Z are from sample 3.

Appendix G (cnt'd)

Table 1: Variables in the Analysis[a]

Sample 1 Variable	Sample 2 Variable	Sample 3 Variable
X10[b]=Dummy variable for warrants, coded 1 for no warrants, 0 otherwise.	Y9[b]= Dummy variable for employment status, coded 1 for unemployed, 0 otherwise.	Z10=Dummy variable for offender-victim category, coded 1 for White defendant vs. White complainant, government agency, 0 otherwise.
X11= Dummy variable for adjustment in prior correctional program, coded 1 for poor, 0 otherwise.	Y10= Dummy variable for warrants, coded 1 for warrants, 0 otherwise.	Z11=Dummy variable for offender-victim category, coded 1 for Black Puerto Rican def. vs. White complainant, gov. agency, 0 otherwise.
X12= Dummy variable for adjustment in prior correctional program, coded 1 for good, 0 otherwise.	Y11= Dummy variable for ethnicity of complainant, coded 1 for White, 0 otherwise.	Z12=Dummy variable for offender-victim category, coded 1 for Black, Puerto Rican def. vs. Black, Puerto Rican complainant, 0 otherwise.
X13= Dummy variable for ethnicity of complainant, coded 1 for White, government agency, 0 otherwise.	Y12= Dummy variable for ethnicity of complainant, coded 1 for Black, 0 otherwise.	
X14= Dummy variable for ethnicity of complainant, coded 1 for Black, 0 otherwise.		

[a]See Chapter III for scaling of the variables.

[b]Variables designated X are from sample 1, variables designated Y are from sample 2 and variables designated Z are from sample 3.

Appendix G (cnt'd)

Table 1: Variables in the Analysis[a]

Sample 1 Variable	Sample 2 Variable	Sample 3 Variable
X15[b]= Dummy variable for ethnicity of complainant, coded 1 for Puerto Rican, 0 otherwise.	Y13= Dummy variable for ethnicity of complainant, coded 1 for Puerto Rican, 0 otherwise.	SOC= Seriousness of orig. charges, coded 1 for crimes against persons, 2 for crimes against property, 3 for victimless crimes.
X16= Dummy variable for offender-victim category, coded 1 for White defendant vs. White complainant, gov. agency, 0 otherwise.	Y14= Dummy variable for offender-victim category, coded 1 for White defendant vs. White complainant, gov. agency, 0 otherwise.	SFC= Seriousness of final charge, coded 1 for crimes against persons, 2 for crimes against property, 3 for victimless crimes.
X17= Dummy variable for offender-victim category, coded 1 for White defendant v. Black, Puerto Rican complainant, 0 otherwise.	Y15= Dummy variable for offender-victim category, coded 1 for White def. vs. Black, Puerto Rican complainant, 0 otherwise.	NA= Number of arrests.

[a]See Chapter III for scaling of the variables.

[b]Variables designated X are from sample 1, variables designated Y are from sample 2 and variables designated Z from sample 3.

203

Appendix G (cnt'd)

Table 1: Variables in the Analysis[a]

Sample 1 Variable	Sample 2 Variable	Sample 3 Variable
X18[b]=Dummy variable for offender-victim category, coded 1 for Black, Puerto Rican defendant vs. White complainant, gov. agency, 0 otherwise.	Y16[b]=Dummy variable for offender-victim category, coded 1 for Black, Puerto Rican defendant vs. White complainant, gov. agency, 0 otherwise.	SPA[b]=Seriousness of prior arrests, coded 1 for crimes against persons, 2 for crimes against property, 3 for victimless crimes, 4 for no prior arrests.
X19=Dummy variable for offender-victim category, coded 1 for Black, Puerto Rican defendant vs. Black, Puerto Rican complainant, 0 otherwise.	Y17=Dummy variable for offender-victim category, coded 1 for Black, Puerto Rican defendant vs. Black, Puerto Rican complainant, 0 otherwise.	DJ= Disposition of judge, coded 1 for jail, 2 for probation, 3 for conditional discharge, 4 for fine, 5 for unconditional discharge.
X20= Dummy variable for pretrial status, coded 1 for remand, 0 otherwise.	Y18= Dummy variable for legal service, coded 1 for legal aid, 0 otherwise.	

[a]See Chapter III for scaling of the variables.

[b]Variables designated X are from sample 1, variables designated Y are from sample 2, and variables designated Z are from sample 3.

204

Appendix G (cnt'd)

Table 1: Variables in the Analysis[a]

Sample 1 Variable	Sample 2 Variable	Sample 3 Variable
$X21^b$=Dummy variable for legal service, coded 1 for legal aid, 0 otherwise.	$Y19^b$=Dummy variable for legal service, coded 1 for legal aid and private lawyer, 0 otherwise.	
$X22$= Interaction of recommendation of probation officer, number of arrests, seriousness of final charge.	$Y20$= Dummy variable for legal aid, coded 1 for private lawyer, 0 otherwise.	
$X23$= Interaction of number of convictions, seriousness of final charge.	$Y21$= Dummy variable for pretrial status, coded 1 for remand, 0 otherwise.	
$X24$= Interaction of remand, promises.	$Y22$= Dummy variable for pretrial status, coded 1 for out, 0 otherwise.	
	$Y23$= Interaction of seriousness of final charge, number of arrests.	

[a] See Chapter III for scaling of the variables.

[b] Variables designated X are from sample 1, variables designated Y from sample 2, and variables designated Z from sample 3.

Appendix G (cnt'd)
Table 1

Variables in the Analysis[a]

Sample 1 Variable	Sample 2 Variable	Sample 3 Variable
X25[b]=Interaction of employment, marital status.	Y24[b]=Interaction of remand, number of arrests, seriousness of final charge, warrants.	
X26=Interaction of promises, warrants.	Y25=Interaction of number of arrests, seriousness of final charge, warrants.	
X27=Interaction of White complainant, Black, Puerto Rican defendant vs. White complainant, gov. agency.	SOC=Seriousness of original charge, coded 1 for crimes against persons, 2 for crimes against property, 3 for victimless crimes.	
X28=Interaction of poor adjustment in prior correctional program, number of arrests, seriousness of final charge.	SFC=Seriousness of final charge, coded 1 for crimes against	

[a]See Chapter III for scaling of the variables.

[b]Variables designated X are from sample 1, variables designated Y from sample 2, and variables designated Z from sample 3.

Appendix G (cnt'd)

Table 1

Variables in the Analysis[a]

Sample 1 Variable	Sample 2 Variable	Sample 3 Variable
X29[b] =Interaction of good adjustment in prior correctional program, number of arrests, seriousness of final charge.	persons, 2 for crimes against property, 3 for victimless crimes.	
X30=Interaction of White defendant, employment.	NA=Number of arrests.	
X31=Interaction of Black defendant, employment.	NC=Number of convictions.	
X32=Interaction of White defendant, number of arrests.	SPA=Seriousness of prior arrests, coded 1 for crimes against persons, 2 for crimes against property, 3 for victimless crimes, 4 for no prior arrests.	
X33=Interaction of Black defendant, number of arrests.	DPC=Disposition of prior convictions, coded 1 for jail, 2 for probation, 3 for conditional, unconditional discharge, fine, 4 for no prior convictions.	

[a]See Chapter III for scaling of the variables.

[b]Variables designated X are from sample 1, variables designated Y from sample 2, and variables designated Z from sample 3.

Appendix G (cnt'd)

Table 1

Variables in the Analysis[a]

Sample 1 Variable	Sample 2 Variable	Sample 3 Variable
SOC[b] =Seriousness of original charge, coded 1 for crimes against persons, 2 for crimes against property, 3 for victimless crimes.	DJ=Disposition of judge, coded 1 for jail, 2 for probation, 3 for conditional discharge, 4 for fine, 5 for unconditional discharge.	
SFC=Seriousness of final charge, coded 1 for crimes against persons, 2 for crimes against property, 3 for victimless crimes.		
NA=Number of arrests.		
NC=Number of convictions.		
SPA=Seriouss of prior arrests, coded 1 for crimes against persons, 2 for crimes against property, 3 for victimless crimes, 4 for		

[a]See Chapter III for scaling of the variables.

[b]Variables designated X are from sample 1, variables designated Y from sample 2, and variables designated Z from sample 3.

Appendix G (con'd)
Table 1
Variables in the Analysis[a]

Sample 1 Variable	Sample 2 Variable	Sample 3 Variable
no prior arrests.		
DPC[b]=Disposition of prior convictions, coded 1 for jail, 2 for probation, 3 for conditional, unconditional discharge, fine, 4 for no prior convictions.		
RPO=Recommendation of the probation officer, coded 1 for jail, 2 for probation, 3 for conditional discharge, 4 for fine, 5 for unconditional discharge.		
DJ=Disposition of judge, coded 1 for jail, 2 for probation, 3 for conditional discharge, 4 for fine, 5 for unconditional discharge.		

[a]See Chapter III for scaling of the variables.

[b]Variables designated X are from sample 1, variables designated Y from sample 2, and variables designated Z from sample 3.

NOTE: In the event of multiple authorship, only the first author named in a journal is cited here.

ABOUT THE AUTHOR

James R. Davis is a probation officer and researcher for the Department of Probation, New York City. He holds a B.A. in history, and an M.A. and Ph.D. in sociology. He has presented papers at national and state sociological associations, and has written in Federal Probation. He also teaches statistics part-time at Baruch College, City University of New York. He is now engaged in writing a book about the science of criminal justice.